# THE G. STANLEY HALL
# LECTURE SERIES

## Volume 1

G. STANLEY HALL, 1844–1924

# THE G. STANLEY HALL LECTURE SERIES

## Volume 1

Edited by
### Ludy T. Benjamin, Jr.
Texas A&M University

## 1980 HALL LECTURERS

### David Elkind
### Gregory A. Kimble
### Walter Mischel
### Jerome L. Singer
### Wilse B. Webb

AMERICAN PSYCHOLOGICAL ASSOCIATION
WASHINGTON, D.C.

Published by the American Psychological Association, Inc.,
1200 Seventeenth Street, N.W., Washington, D.C. 20036
Copyright © 1981 by the American Psychological Association.
All rights reserved.

Library of Congress Catalog Card No.: 81-66984

ISBN: 0-912704-36-5

Copies may be ordered from:
Order Department
American Psychological Association
1200 Seventeenth Street, N.W.
Washington, D.C. 20036

*Printed in the United States of America.*

# CONTENTS

93270

# PREFACE

The inaugural G. Stanley Hall Lectures were given at the 1980 meeting of the American Psychological Association in Montreal, Canada, and are printed here in a form close to that of the original presentations. The publication of those lectures in this volume marks the second step in a new program of the APA, a program designed principally for instructors of introductory psychology.

The idea for the lecture series grew out of a meeting of APA's Committee on Undergraduate Education (CUE) in March, 1979. During a discussion of needs for undergraduate instructors, attention focused on the introductory course as a survey of the diverse areas that constitute the field of psychology. In that course the instructor is faced with the awesome task of covering as many as 20 to 25 topical areas. Adding to the difficulty of that task is the fact that few instructors, if any, can claim familiarity with the current literature in more than a half dozen of those areas. The committee discussed ways that APA might aid the instructor of introductory psychology and settled on a plan for a special lecture series to be presented at the annual meeting of APA. A proposal was prepared for review by APA's Education and Training Board (the parent board of CUE) and for review by the Committee on Continuing Education, since, with its purpose of content updating, the lecture series was also viewed as a continuing education program. In addition, copies of the proposal were sent to a number of individuals identified with undergraduate education in psychology, including the leadership of APA's Division 2, the Division of the Teaching of Psychology.

The proposal outlined the lecture series as a five-year program covering five different topics each year. Twenty topical areas were identified as standard subjects for course coverage including personality, physiological psychology, motivation, emotion, developmental psychology, and 15 others. The proposal called for coverage of four of these topics each year with a fifth lecture to be designated as a special topic chosen each year to reflect contemporary interests. Thus the program would consist of 25 lectures covering different areas over a five-year period. At the end of the first cycle, that is, in the sixth year, the program would begin again with the four standard topics covered in the initial year of the series plus the selected special topic. Coverage in each lecture would emphasize the literature of the previous five years, a time period that seemed reasonable for meaningful integration of a circumscribed body of literature and the time frame planned for the subsequent presentations of that topic.

The proposal outlined criteria for the selection of appropriate lecturers. Since the principal goal of the series was to aid teachers of introductory psychology, emphasis was placed on the selection of lecturers who (a) were experts in their particular content area, (b) had a strong interest in teaching psychology, and (c) had experience in teaching introductory psychology and an understanding of the special problems inherent in teaching a survey course in introductory psychology. This last point was judged to be especially important if the lectures were to effectively meet the needs of the intended audience.

Making its way through the governance structure of APA, the proposal for the lecture series was approved by the Education and Training Board, the Board of Convention Affairs, and the Board of Directors. As approved, the lecture series was to be coordinated with the other continuing education activities of APA at the annual meeting. The five lectures would each be scheduled for two hours, with the second hour devoted to audience–lecturer discussion. The five-year cycle of topics and the selection of lecturers would be determined by a special advisory committee consisting of two members appointed from the Committee on Undergraduate Education, two members from the

Committee on Continuing Education, and two members appointed by Division 2. Administrative responsibilities for the program would be handled by the APA Educational Affairs Office in conjunction with the Convention Affairs Office.

As suggested in the original proposal, the lecture program was named the G. Stanley Hall Lecture Series, chiefly to acknowledge Hall's role as founder of the American Psychological Association. Such a designation seemed especially appropriate given Hall's considerable interest in teaching and his diverse interests in psychology, which included perception, child study, mental testing, emotion, hypnosis, prejudice, aging, industrial psychology, and psychoanalysis. Hall has been honored in many other ways as well. There are distinguished professorships in his name at Clark University and at Johns Hopkins University, public schools have been named in his honor, and an annual award presented by APA's Division 7 (Developmental Psychology) also bears his name.

One of the concerns in establishing the series was that the material reach as many instructors as possible. Obviously, many individuals interested in the lectures would be unable to attend the annual meeting. Thus a decision was made to publish the lectures each year as an APA separate, a decision that brought this volume into existence. While the lectures are aimed principally at introductory psychology instructors, they should prove useful to other instructors or to researchers and practitioners outside of academia who view these papers as a way to keep informed on the topics that are the core of psychology.

The enthusiastic reception accorded the lectures at the APA meeting in Montreal initiated a successful beginning for the series. I hope this book will be as well received and that readers will find the content and pedagogical suggestions of substantial import. Topics covered this year are learning, language and thought, personality, clinical psychology, and states of consciousness.

The initial paper by Gregory Kimble looks at a wealth of literature on learning and memory in terms of a model focusing on biological and cognitive constraints on those processes. Emphasizing these organismic variables, Kimble integrates a number of seemingly disparate topics through illustrations of the role of biological and psychological (principally cognitive) characteristics as determinants of what the organism is capable of learning and remembering. Into this analysis he weaves the topics of preparedness, taste aversion, fear conditioning, autoshaping, instinctive drift, negative reinforcement, language acquisition in humans and other primates, learned helplessness, memory capacity, encoding, modes of representation, state-dependent learning, and the maintenance of knowledge. Such a list may leave the reader wondering what is left! Kimble's paper is far-reaching in its implications for interpretation in psychology and draws heavily on the data base of the past five years. It is a stimulating account that at best should offer instructors an integrative framework for teaching the subject matter of learning or at worst provide them a means to argue against traditional views in the field.

The second paper, by David Elkind, is a treatment of recent research in language development and cognition. This review of the literature covers research areas that constitute major trends in the field and emphasizes social cognition, metacognition, and a reconceptualization of research on role taking. In language development he looks at children's use of orientational terms, at language situations, at bilingual learning, at ape language, and at studies of individual differences. In his treatment of social cognition, Elkind discusses the research on children's (a) social conceptions, (b) scientific thinking, (c) conceptions regarding the causes, prevention, and treatment of illness, and (d) conceptions of the clergy. These studies are treated as a basis for understanding educational research and programs that deal with the role of the adult in the child's learning and development. This paper, like Kimble's, focuses on controversy, and Elkind offers some suggestions about the way controversy can be used to teach students about the workings of science.

In the third paper, Walter Mischel discusses four traditions in the field of personality that he feels are important to cover in the introductory course: the measurement of intelligence, the measurement of traits and types, underlying psychodynamic motives, and a comparison of behavioral and humanistic approaches. He suggests teaching these traditions by applying each to an analysis of the same case material, thus illustrating the strengths and weaknesses of each approach. Mischel focuses on uses and misuses of the trait approach in personality, contrasting the needs for making generalizations about the individual "on the whole" with the need for an understanding of what the person is doing in context. He describes recent developments in the study of traits and types such as the work on prototypicality or "typical people" as an example of person characteristics and research on scripts as situational determinants. Throughout this paper, Mischel attempts to show that the study of personality necessarily depends on an assessment of a host of variables such as an individual's expectancies, competencies, and encoding strategies, to name a few, and that such an approach is important for psychology as a unified science.

Jerome Singer's paper surveys recent developments in clinical intervention with the individual client, stressing problem-focused treatment methods. This review spans the gamut of therapeutic techniques from psychodynamic methods to systematic desensitization to assertiveness training. Common to a number of the techniques discussed is a reliance on the imagery capacities of the client, a topic that receives considerable attention in Singer's paper. Since most therapy takes place in settings far removed from the actual problem environments, focus on imaginal abilities enhances the potential for generalization of therapy to those problem settings. Descriptions of Meichenbaum's work with impulsiveness and Zimbardo's work with shyness are included as illustrations of the potential of imagery techniques in producing behavior change. In addition to a review of treatment methods, Singer includes a section on the emerging field of behavioral medicine and a final section evaluating the effectiveness of psychotherapy.

The final paper, this year's special topic, is by sleep researcher Wilse Webb and is entitled "The Return of Consciousness." Webb's introductory remarks trace the course of consciousness from the days of William James and E. B. Titchener through the time of radical behaviorism to the present. His title reveals the outcome of that historical search. Consciousness is back, and Webb sees this return as signaling the beginning of a paradigmatic revolution, a revolution that means psychology must deal not only with behavior but with experience as well. Following the format of most contemporary introductory psychology texts, Webb discusses sleep and dreams, drug states, hypnosis, and meditation as states of consciousness. He deals with each of these topical areas in a final section of his paper that describes classroom demonstrations and provides other teaching tips.

The five papers that comprise this initial volume in the G. Stanley Hall Lecture Series differ other than in topic of coverage. While they all focus on the most recent literature, one emphasizes a few trends in considerable detail while another mentions many current investigations. The papers also differ widely in terms of their recommendations for classroom activities and demonstrations; some of the papers give these activities substantial emphasis, yet other papers provide little material of this kind. Still, these papers have much in common, and it is this commonality that is at the heart of the lecture series. These papers are more than mere reviews of the past five years' literature, they are integrative accounts of that literature. Each attempts to place its content area in the context of a survey introductory course, recognizing the limitations of coverage and understanding inherent in such a course. I hope instructors of psychology, as well as others in our field, will find this series of benefit.

This volume originated with the selection of the G. Stanley Hall Lecturers, a task accomplished by a special advisory committee composed of Charles Brewer, Douglas Candland, David Cole, Irene Goldenberg, Joseph Hasazi, and Charles Morris. Their efforts are greatly appreciated.

The editor also wishes to express gratitude to Emily Davidson, Jack Nation, John Riskind, and Steven M. Smith for their comments on earlier versions of this initial set of G. Stanley Hall Lectures.

Finally, special thanks are extended to Kathleen D. Lowman, of the American Psychological Association's Educational Affairs Office, whose many efforts helped to make the G. Stanley Hall Lecture Series and this publication a reality.

Ludy T. Benjamin, Jr.

GREGORY A. KIMBLE

# BIOLOGICAL AND COGNITIVE CONSTRAINTS ON LEARNING

G regory A. Kimble is professor and chair of the Department of Psychology at Duke University. He has distinguished himself as a major contributor to the growth of psychology through his roles as teacher, researcher, writer, editor, and administrator. Since receiving his doctorate from the University of Iowa in 1945, Dr. Kimble has held faculty positions at the following Universities: Brown, Missouri, Yale, North Carolina, Harvard, Colorado, California, Hawaii, and Duke.

Kimble's bibliography numbers more than 100 items, including six books. His first book was *Teaching Tips: A Guide Book for the Beginning Teacher,* published in 1953 (with W. McKeachie). Three years later he published the first edition of his *Principles of General Psychology*, an extremely popular introductory psychology text now in its fifth edition (with N. Garmezy and E. Zigler).

His identification as one of the leading authorities in the field of learning has earned Kimble a number of honors including membership in the prestigious Society of Experimental Psychologists, fellow status in four divisions of the American Psychological Association and the American Association for the Advancement of Science, and the presidency of APA's Division of Experimental Psychology and the

Rocky Mountain Psychological Association. He has been a NATO Fellow at Cambridge University and editor of *Psychological Monographs,* and he presently serves as editor of the *Journal of Experimental Psychology: General* and as a member of the Board of Directors of APA.

His experience and familiarity with diverse areas of psychology uniquely qualify Kimble to make the journey described in this paper. As its title implies, the paper focuses on biological characteristics and cognitive states as organismic variables affecting learning. Most important, Kimble's paper provides a conceptual model for integrating and understanding much of the literature in learning and related areas.

# BIOLOGICAL AND COGNITIVE CONSTRAINTS ON LEARNING

I n assessing recent developments in the field of learning it is useful to begin by asking whether these changes have been revolutionary or evolutionary in nature and whether they require a revised view of the field as a whole or merely the assimilation of new information to familiar patterns of thought. The beleaguered teacher of introductory psychology will be relieved to learn that the changes have been evolutionary; it is not necessary quite yet to scrap last year's lectures and create new ones in order to portray some cataclysmic paradigm shift. The most impressive developments in the past half decade have provided several interesting new demonstrations of well-known phenomena, occasional practical applications of traditional ideas, and now and then, important additions to our understanding of the effects of recognized variables. These developments, though highly significant, do not represent the overthrow of traditional ways of thinking about the learning process.

Several of the people whose work is cited in this paper made helpful comments on a preliminary draft: Richard C. Anderson, Harry Bahrick, Gordon H. Bower, William G. Chase, Anders Ericsson, John Garcia, Steven F. Maier, Susan Roth, Martin E. P. Seligman, and Herbert S. Terrace.

I especially wish to thank Shari Alexander for her careful work in preparing the manuscript.

This point may be worth an additional word or two, because it is the fashion in some quarters these days to view our most recent history as the rejection of stimulus–response (S–R) theorizing, where the S–R viewpoint is seen as (a) analytic to the point of treating stimuli in terms of specific physical energies and responses in terms of specific twitchings of muscles and squirtings of glands, (b) environmental to the point of leaving the organism either empty or totally out of the picture, and (c) mechanistic to the point of reducing all human activity to the automatic operation of thoughtless reflex processes. Probably the most common reaction to such a description is an indignant one: Such theorizing *should* be given up and the sooner, the better!

My own present view is that this reaction is based on a confusion, which many of us once shared, between theoretical accomplishments and theoretical ambitions. Although a psychology of the very distant future might be like the spectre of S–R psychology just described, no past or present treatment of learning actually possessed all of these features. Most important, every S–R psychology put forward has always been an S–O–R psychology, where "O" is the organism conceived in terms sometimes concrete and physiological, sometimes abstract and conceptual. The properties assigned to O place important limitations on the learning process. The biological characteristics of the organism determine whether a bit of learning is easy or even possible for members of a given species. Psychological factors, particularly the set of the learner and the interpretation or meaning placed on a situation, play a similar role. Recent developments in the field of learning have emphasized these limitations—hence the title of this paper.

## Biological Constraints

The best known of the biological constraints on learning is that demonstrated by the classical conditioning of aversions to certain tastes. Revusky and Garcia (1970) introduce the basic idea using a homey example:

> [Suppose while you are reading this account] . . . you find
> $100 on the floor. Presumably this functions as a reward for you.
> The $100 was left by an insane billionaire experimenter because,
> two hours ago at lunch, [for the first time in your life ] you ate

gooseberry pie for dessert instead of your usual apple pie. The experimenter wanted to increase the future probability that you would eat gooseberry pie.

It is very unlikely that this experiment will be successful unless you are actually told the connection between consumption of gooseberry pie and receipt of the $100. . . .

Let us now change . . . our thought experiment: [Two hours after the lunch with the gooseberry pie] you are reading this paper and suddenly you become sick. Since the gooseberry pie was new to you, you would probably conclude that the pie caused the illness. . . .

Thus associations over long delays must be explained in terms of natural restraints on the process of associative learning.

The message that Revusky and Garcia wish to convey is that the human organism is prepared to develop associations between tastes and sickness. Or, to use Thorndike's terminology, it is as if tastes and sickness belong together. Tastes and monetary rewards do not belong together. The human organism is at least unprepared, and probably contraprepared, to develop associations between events of the latter type.

## Equipotentiality Versus Preparedness

This *principle of preparedness* is to be contrasted with what has been called the *premise of equipotentiality,* according to which associations are formed with equal ease between any events that can be associated at all. This premise was explicit in Pavlov's 1927 book and was put forth with characteristic bluntness by Kimble (1956) 30 years later:

A great deal of [research on conditioning] may be summarized by saying that it indicated that just about any activity of which the organism is capable can be conditioned, and that these responses can be conditioned to any stimulus that the organism can perceive. (p. 195)

By 1980 there were half a thousand reports in the literature that proved this pronouncement wrong.

One of the cleanest of these demonstrations (Garcia & Koelling, 1966) showed that rats are prepared to associate tastes with sickness and exteroceptive stimuli with punishment by electric shock but that they are not prepared to make the opposite associations: tastes with shock and exteroceptive stimulation with sickness. In this experiment, rats were allowed to drink a saccharin-flavored solution. Each lick at the drinking tube, however, produced both a click and a flash of light as well as the sweet taste. In this way the investigators created a situation that made the click–light combination the consequence of licking, just as tastes normally are.

Following this preliminary experience some of the rats were made sick with x-irradiation; others were punished with electric shock. Then, as a test, the rats were allowed to drink again. But now the two forms of stimulation were separated. On alternate days the water was either sweet with saccharin but dark and silent (the click and light were turned off) or bright and noisy but tasteless (the water no longer contained saccharin). The amount drunk under these two conditions depended upon the types of punishment the rats had experienced. If the rats had received x-irradiation they avoided the sweet-dark-silent water but consumed normal amounts of the bright-noisy-tasteless water. If they had received electric shock the results were the exact opposite. These rats had developed an aversion to the bright-noisy-tasteless water but drank their usual amounts of the sweet-dark-silent water (see Figure 1).

Because so many important variables were controlled, the experiment just described is a particularly neat demonstration of the phenomenon of prepared associations. Other research has made the following points, which, owing to space limitations, can only be summarized here:

1. Although the matter is somewhat controversial, the learning involved in the development of taste aversion is a variety of classical conditioning.

2. Such conditioning can take place with impressively long CS (taste)–US (sickness) intervals, two hours or more, and with only a single pairing of conditioned stimulus and unconditioned stimulus. Conditioned aversions can be weakened by extinction but are strongly resistant to the process.

3. A wide variety of tastes and a similarly wide variety of ways of producing sickness can be effective.

4. There are species differences in the processes by which these aversions are developed. If quail are made sick after the ingestion of sweet blue water it is the blueness rather than the sweetness that is aversive later. An early interpretation of this result was that the blue

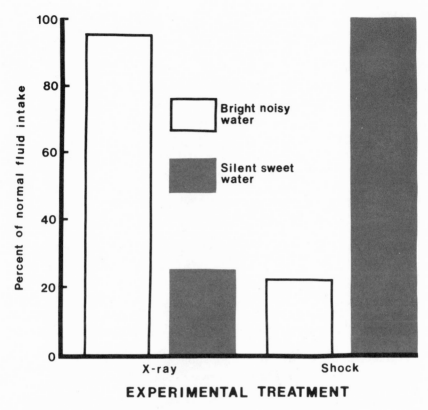

**Figure 1.** X-ray induced sickness is associated with taste; shock-induced pain is associated with external stimulation.

predominated in the control of the aversion because, as is well known, birds are highly visual animals. More recent research (Garcia & Rusiniak, 1980) has shown, however, that the sweet taste contributes to the process. Conditioning to blue tasteless water does not lead to an aversion. It is as if the sweet taste potentiates the effectiveness of blue.

5. One of the most important variables determining the ease with which taste aversions can be conditioned is stimulus novelty. Experience with a taste prior to the occasion when the animal is made sick tends to inoculate the subject against the development of an aversion to that taste.

## Application to Human Fear Conditioning

Evidence that something like the principle of preparedness might apply to human fear conditioning has existed for at least 50 years. In 1920 Watson and Rayner reported the landmark study in which they conditioned the child Albert to fear a white rat. Later assessments were to include this study in the collection of evidence favoring the premise of equipotentiality, in spite of certain very damaging details in the evidence. In 1961, just five years after Kimble's pronouncement in favor of that premise, we find him writing as follows:

> Attempts to repeat the Watson and Rayner study were not always successful and C. W. Valentine (1930) presented evidence to suggest that fears might be much more easily conditioned to furry objects, such as a caterpillar or a rat, than to others, such as a pair of opera glasses. (pp. 424–425)

Much more recently, Öhman and his colleagues (Öhman, Fredrikson, Hugdahl, & Rimmö, 1976) have demonstrated the correctness of this view. These investigators conditioned the galvanic skin response (GSR), which these days is more often called the electrodermal response (EDR), of human subjects to three different classes of conditioned stimuli: pictures of snakes and spiders, circles and triangles, and flowers and mushrooms. The unconditioned stimulus was electric shock. The ease of conditioning, especially as measured by resistance to extinction, was in the order in which the classes of stimuli were just listed: best to snakes and spiders, next best to circles and triangles, poorest to flowers and mushrooms.

If one thinks of the conventional laboratory stimuli—the circles and triangles—as neutral stimuli, these results suggest that people are prepared to develop phobic reactions to snakes and spiders and are contraprepared to develop them to flowers and mushrooms. Öhman and his associates also make the point that since the GSR component affected is the component associated with orienting behavior, the conditioning procedure affects the meaning of the pictures: The pictures become fearful pictures—snakes and spiders most fearful, flowers and mushrooms least.

All of which raises a question: If fears are so easy to condition to fuzzy, furry stimuli, are not stuffed plush toys like teddy bears dangerous to the health of the nation's infants? Would we not be better advised to concentrate on rattles, pacifiers, and teething rings? If one takes this question more seriously than it sounds, as I do, the answer may lie in the inoculating effects of stimulus familiarity. At least the results of studies of taste aversion suggest such a possibility. Perhaps generations of parents have discovered that experience with cuddly cloth toys staves off the development of phobic reactions to harmless animals and hairy relatives. On the whole, immunity to such fears would appear to be adaptive.

*Prepared Responses*

One way to summarize the studies just presented is to say that they demonstrate the existence of certain sympathies between predictive *stimuli* and reinforcers that make associations between them easy to establish. Let me now shift the emphasis just a bit to make the point that similar sympathies exist between *responses* and reinforcers. For example, anyone who has studied operant conditioning in the laboratory knows that it is very easy to train pigeons to peck illuminated keys for food or rats to press levers for food but that—while possible —it is very difficult to train these same animals to make the *same responses* to avoid electic shock. The unfolding story has added a great deal to our understanding of constraints on learning, and separate chapters on positive and negative reinforcers describe somewhat different features of the plot.

*Autoshaping.* If the key in the Skinner box for pigeons lights up and food is made available soon thereafter, pigeons train themselves to peck the key for food (Brown & Jenkins, 1968). This easy learning occurs because a response very similar to the response employed when the pigeon eats is the response being learned. The effect of this variable is very powerful. If an autoshaped response is put on an *omission schedule,* according to which a peck guarantees that food will not follow, the pigeon nevertheless continues to peck.

Additional evidence of the way in which biological factors contribute to learning comes from studies that at first seemed to require quite a different interpretation. Many years ago Skinner (1948) described an important experiment on superstitious behavior in the pigeon. The pigeons were placed in the Skinner box, and the food hopper was opened at fixed intervals, allowing access to grain no matter what the pigeons did. There was no actual contingency between any response the birds could make and reinforcement. Under these circumstances the pigeons developed individual patterns of "ritualistic" behavior, which they performed as though they believed that food was contingent on these particular responses. These superstitious responses consisted of such things as circling the chamber, bowing, flapping the wings, and stretching the neck, all in ceremonial sequence.

Skinner's interpretation of these actions was that the pigeon repeated whatever it happened to be doing when the hopper opened. Its chance activities of the moment, reinforced in this way, were automatically strengthened and organized into a chain of reactions that the pigeon performed to bridge the temporal gap from one reinforcement to the next.

At first blush these data seem to lend powerful support to the principle of equipotentiality. Reinforcement apparently dictated the selection of whatever movement the pigeon was making as it was offered. Later work was to show that although there is more truth to this interpretation than the work on biological constraints may suggest, important qualifications still need to be made.

Staddon and Simmelhag (1971) repeated Skinner's experiment on superstition, but they made much more detailed observations of the pigeon's responses. They obtained the same results as Skinner had, but with one important addition: The ritualistic sequences of behavior always ended with a feeding response. This response was pecking in every pigeon except one, whose reaction was to move its head toward the food hopper. Such behavior seemed to occur more and more dependably as training progressed.

At this point it may be worth introducing a couple of other cases in which a more biological interpretation should replace an original account presented in terms of learning and reinforcement. The first of these is the old example from Neal Miller (1948) that stood for years as a laboratory demonstration of the psychoanalytic phenomenon of displacement. Since such an interpretation still persists in some introductory textbooks, a 30+ -year regression may not be out of order here. We might begin once more with a quote from Kimble (1956):

> An experimental demonstration of displacement . . . has been reported by Miller. He put two rats into a cage with an electrifiable grid as the floor. Then he turned on the shock and turned it off only when the rats assumed an upright, face-to-face

position as if they were fighting. *Since the organism will learn any response which is rewarded* this reaction was soon learned. Then Miller removed one of the rats from the cage and substituted for it a small rubber doll. When the shock was turned on now, the remaining rat attacked the rubber doll. (p. 352, italics added)

The discussion goes on to implicate the process of stimulus generalization in this demonstration. This time it took Kimble (1968) 12 years to see the error of his ways. Referring to the learning-reinforcement-stimulus generalization explanation as "entirely reasonable," he went on to say:

As it happens this entirely reasonable explanation is wrong. . . . An extensive series of studies . . . have made it quite clear that aggression is an unlearned reaction to pain, that organisms of many species will attack another organism, or even an inanimate object in response to the onset of shock. (p. 44)

The second example also has a long history, but the denouement is much more recent. In 1946, Guthrie and Horton published their study of cats escaping from a puzzle box. In their report they emphasized the fact that the cats tended to use identical movements when they tilted the pole in the box that achieved release. They interpreted this result to support Guthrie's hypothesis that what an organism learns when it learns anything is a detailed set of movements followed by a dramatic change in the situation.

In 1979, Moore and Stuttard published a note in *Science* that puts quite another light on the matter. In brief, Moore and Stuttard showed that the movements produced by the cat, while stereotyped as Guthrie and Horton had found, were actually species-typical greeting responses probably directed at the experimenters, who were present in the room. In fact, Moore and Stuttard showed that they could turn these responses on and off by the simple expedient of having an audience present in the room or absent.

*Instinctive drift.* Sometimes the innate dispositions of organisms serve not to further the purposes of experimenters but to frustrate them. This 20-year-old example, the dancing chicken of Breland and Breland (1961), will serve to introduce the point:

The chicken walks over about 3 feet, pulls a rubber loop on a small box which starts a repeated auditory stimulus pattern (a four-note tune). The chicken then steps up onto an 18-inch, slightly raised disc, thereby closing a timer switch, and scratches vigorously, round and round, over the disc for 15 seconds, at the rate of about two scratches per second until the automatic feeder fires in the retaining compartment. The chicken goes into the compartment to eat, thereby automatically shutting the door. The popular interpetation of this behavior pattern is that the chicken has turned on the "juke box" and "dances."

The development of this behavioral exhibit was wholly unplanned. In the attempt to create quite another type of demonstration which required a chicken simply to stand on a platform for 12–15 seconds, we found that over 50% developed a very strong and pronounced scratch pattern, which tended to increase in persistence as the time interval was lengthened. (Another 25% or so developed other behaviors—pecking at spots, etc.) However, we were able to change our plans so as to make use of the scratch pattern, and the result was the "dancing chicken" exhibit described above.

In this exhibit the only real contingency for reinforcement is that the chicken must depress the platform for 15 seconds. In the course of a performing day (about 3 hours for each chicken) a chicken may turn out over 10,000 unnecessary, virtually identical responses. (pp. 681–682)

The Brelands call this phenomenon *instinctive drift,* a process that they describe this way:

Here we have animals, after having been conditioned to a specific learned response, gradually drifting into behaviors that are entirely different from those which were conditioned. Moreover, it can easily be seen that these particular behaviors to which the animals drift are clear-cut examples of instinctive behaviors having to do with the natural food-getting behaviors of the particular species. (p. 683)

*Species-specific defense reactions.* The very last experiment I ever did on avoidance conditioning never got beyond the pilot stage. It was an attempt to train rats to press a lever and then release it after the presentation of a light stimulus to avoid electric shock. The press–release contingency was introduced in order to preclude the possibility of the animals' learning to lean on the bar, keeping it permanently depressed, and thus making it impossible to administer another trial. After 15–20 unsuccessful attempts with as many subjects, I gave up.

Not a single animal learned the bar-pressing response. Early in the experiment most of them produced that reaction, but they soon gave it up. Eventually all of the rats reacted to the light by crouching and cowering immobile in a corner of the conditioning apparatus.

That was sometime in the early 1950s. Guided by then-current Hullian learning theory, I concluded that the time it took for the lever to return to the released position after it had been pressed ($^1/_{20}$ of a second or so) was enough time for some other response than lever pressing to occur and to be reinforced by shock reduction. It occurred to me that such reasoning might require a rethinking of Hull's delay-of-reinforcement postulate and that possibly reinforcement could be delayed indefinitely if, somehow, one could find a way to protect responses from such interferences.

In 1980 these once-radical ideas no longer seem strange. The fact that the rats learned to crouch and cower instead of to press the lever in my aborted experiment shows, as Bolles (1970) has stressed, that animals find it very easy to acquire *species-specific defense reactions* in avoidance learning. Crouching, cowering, and freezing are very characteristic fear reactions in the rat, and the fact that rats in my preliminary experiments produced them instead of lever pressing would not come as a surprise these days. There are even fragments of evidence for such influences in human fear conditioning. Samelson (1980), for example, picked up the point, missed by all of us for years, that Little Albert in the Watson and Rayner experiment typically responded by plunging his thumb into his mouth and sucking it. Thumb sucking, of course, is a high-probability reaction to fear in many children. Also, the idea that reinforcers are effective over time spans during which responses can be protected from interferences has been proposed by several authors.

A major point at which current thinking differs from the ideas I entertained in the early 1950s concerns the process of reinforcement in avoidance learning. The earlier theory was stated in terms of pain or fear reduction; it is more common now to refer to safety signals and to say that reinforcement for avoidant behavior derives from the effects of such signals, some of which are feedback stimuli from responding that tell the animal a situation is now safe (e.g., Rescorla & LoLordo, 1965).

While we are on the question of the nature of reinforcement for avoidant responses, I would like to go a bit beyond my charge for this paper and deal with a minor issue that has not been settled in the last five years but may be in the next five. At least I hope so. When Ludy Benjamin wrote to me about my participation in the G. Stanley Hall Lectures he suggested that in the discussion period I might have to deal with pedagogical problems in the field of learning. For example, he said someone might ask, "I have trouble explaining the concept of negative reinforcement to my students; do you have a way of getting the idea across?" My reaction to this question is that such troubles are the just desserts of those who use the concept in a curiously illogical way. To quote one culprit who shall remain nameless, "The reinforcing event in avoidance learning has always been considered to be a negative reinforcer, i.e., avoidance acquisition has always been attributed to the reduction of fear or the removal of an aversive CS." Faced with that statement five years from now and asked to make sense of it to a student, I hope one might respond this way:

> The statement you mention used to be a fairly common way of speaking but it led to hopeless confusion between reinforcers, which are stimulus events, and the process of reinforcement, which is a concept. These days we speak in terms that are more nearly those of Thorndike. Positive reinforcers—food, money, and praise are good examples—are things that an organism does nothing to avoid, often doing such things as will obtain or perpetuate them. Negative reinforcers—electric shock, spankings, and criticism are good examples—are things that the organism does nothing to obtain or perpetuate, often doing such things as will prevent or remove them. As you can see, the definitions of positive and negative reinforcement are operational definitions. These operations give events that we usually call rewards a positive sign, in the algebraic sense of positive; events which we call punishment earn negative signs in the same sense.
>
> Another way in which algebraic notation is useful in getting across the essential point is that we can give a positive sign to the administration of a reinforcer and a negative sign to the withholding of one. After that the algebraic rules of multiplying positive and negative quantities are all we need to arrive at the modern definitions: Positive reinforcement is either the delivery of a positive reinforcer or the withholding of a negative reinforcer. Multiplying positive by positive in the first case and negative by negative in the second case both give positive products. Negative reinforcement is either the delivery of a negative reinforcer or the withholding of a positive one, both multiplications yielding negative products. These definitions make our technical terminology

correspond to common experience and prevent the necessity of our having to deal in such absurdities as calling the safety one feels after escaping from a gang of thugs a negative reinforcer.

Figure 2 presents this analysis graphically. Instructors should note that this analysis differs greatly from the way these terms are used in some introductory texts.

**Treatment of Reinforcer**

|  |  | Deliver (+) | Withhold (−) |
|---|---|---|---|
| **Type of Reinforcer** | **Positive (+)** | (+) X (+)<br>Positive<br>Reinforcement | (−) X (+)<br>Negative<br>Reinforcement |
|  | **Negative (−)** | (+) X (−)<br>Negative<br>Reinforcement | (−) X (−)<br>Positive<br>Reinforcement |

**Figure 2.** The algebraic definitions of positive and negative reinforcement.

Another way to put the point just made is to say that students are semantically contraprepared to understand or even learn associations that do not seem to belong together, such as negative reinforcement and escape from fear. This observation puts us back into the mainstream of our discussion.

*Language acquisition.* Given the importance of language in human life, it would be astonishing if God or evolution had left the control of the process entirely up to the uncertainties of training. As every parent and teacher knows, training too often fails to produce the intended result. There is, in fact, substantial evidence that the acquisition of language is guided by powerful biological forces (Lenneberg, 1972). There is space here only to indicate the *types* of evidence that exist for this assertion.

First, the earliest vocalizations of infants, the raw materials out of which language develops, are largely independent of experience. They are the same in all cultures and follow the same pattern in the children of deaf parents as in the children of parents who have normal hearing (see Figure 3).

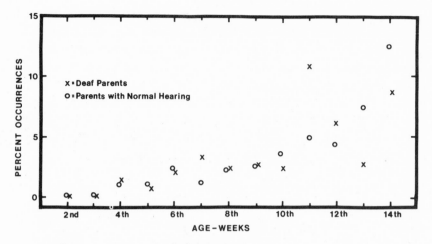

**Figure 3.** The pattern of language development is the same in the early weeks of life in the children of deaf and hearing parents.

Second, language skill is strongly influenced by heredity. The routine finding (Kimble, Garmezy, & Zigler, 1980, p. 217) that verbal intelligence has a coefficient of heritability of about .60 is one indication. Another is that specific abnormalities in language development have a concordance rate of about 90% in identical monozygotic twins as opposed to 40% in fraternal dizygotic twins.

Finally, there are neuroanatomical data that tie language development quite firmly to the development of localized function in the brain. In most adults language is served by a number of specialized areas in the brain. This specialization develops with age. If damage occurs to the areas of the brain that normally serve linguistic functions, the consequences depend upon the age at which the damage occurs. Before the age of two, language is not apt to be much affected. From two to four damage usually produces temporary aphasia from which a child will recover. With increasing age the prognosis becomes increasingly gloomy. Damage in the teens usually produces a permanent deficiency.

These three lines of evidence together make a strong case for language as a biologically prepared response easily mastered by the human organism if given even a minimal opportunity to do so. Such evidence also raises a question: Is language a purely human biological accomplishment, or might we not expect it also to appear in our nearest Darwinian neighbor, the chimpanzee?

The first thing to say about this question is that it tends to bring out the worst in those for whom the answer is important. On the one hand there are the sentimental anthropomorphists who answer in the affirmative and maintain that we are on the verge of being able to share the apes' most personal thoughts, a relationship they probably see as reciprocal. On the other hand there are the anthropo-elitists who say "no," that human beings are a category apart from other forms of animal life and that the uniqueness of human linguistic skill is the best evidence for this conclusion.

If we are forced to take sides in this debate, the most recent data, as well as one fact from the earliest research, urge the acceptance of the latter position. The old, well-established fact is that whatever language the chimpanzee acquires is acquired with enormous difficulty. This is in sharp contrast to the human child, who seems only to require exposure to a linguistic environment—no special training, no special schedules of reinforcement, no special motivational conditions—to master a language. In most cases it is the child's parents who supply this linguistic environment. Doing so, they serve not as trainers of, but as models for, language development. The role played by parents in fostering language acquisition is like the role parents play in socialization and personality development. The examples they set are far more important than the reinforcers they withhold or deliver.

The most recent data (Terrace, 1979) indicate that the linguistic accomplishments of the chimpanzee are probably fewer than we believed a few years ago. Specifically, it now seems quite unlikely that either syntactic competence or the use of language in novel combinations has been demonstrated in the chimpanzee. The syntactic structures used by the chimpanzee are very simple and probably imitations of the experimenter's syntax at that. Terrace has shown that chimpanzees have an unattractive disposition to interrupt their trainers and to copy the trainers' utterances, thus producing their syntax. The creative combinations now seem easily explained as the unconnected production of two "words" appropriate to the context. Thus Washoe's creation of "water-bird" upon seeing a duck can be explained as the production of two responses "water" and "bird" in a situation where they would be expected.

On the other hand, things are never that simple in psychology. While going through the details of Terrace's article, it occurred to me that even his data contained some slight evidence for simple syntax in the chimpanzee. It could be that it is a mistake to put ourselves in the position of making language an all-or-none talent that the chimpanzee either has or doesn't. Perhaps the chimp has 5% (or some such small percentage) of the potential for using syntax that a human being does. Such an estimate would not be out of line with impressions I gleaned from the Terrace data. Rumbaugh and Savage-Rumbaugh (1980) seem to favor an interpretation of that type.

## Cognitive Constraints

The recent accomplishments just described were built on themes developed in the 1960s and very early 1970s. The same period also saw important developments in the cognitive interpretation of learning that seem even more dramatic in perspective. During these years many psychologists of learning who had reputations as rock-hard S–R theorists were turning their research energies to topics that would have been verboten a decade or two earlier. This did not mean that these psychologists had turned soft headed; rather, in every case, the outcomes of research had forced them toward a more cognitive position. In the field of classical conditioning Spence (1963) began a series of studies that recognized the importance of cognitive factors in eyelid conditioning. Grant (1968) wrote on the effects of adding signaling properties to the CS. Grice and Hunter (1964) did a very important study showing that a within-subjects manipulation of CS intensity in which the subjects could make comparisons had a greater effect than a between-subjects manipulation in which they could not. Kimble's (1967) presidential address to Division 3 of the APA was on attitudinal factors in eyelid conditioning, and later on, he and Perlmuter (Kimble & Perlmuter, 1970) wrote on "the problem of volition" in terms that involved conditioned responses.

Elsewhere during this period Amsel (1967) was using the concept of mediation to account for the effects of frustration on instrumental behavior. The Kendlers (Kendler & Kendler, 1968) found the same concept useful in explaining species and age differences in performance on their reversal and nonreversal shift discrimination problems.

In 1964, the publication of McGovern's dissertation on interference theory brought the S–R interpretation of human verbal learning and memory to the peak of its development. Within a few years, however, there would be demonstrations that problems existed for this theory even in the context of paired-associate learning, where it works best. A major problem is that interference theory makes specific S–R pairs the unit of analysis, whereas subjects are able to deal with whole lists of responses, for example, to suppress them (Postman & Stark, 1969). In other contexts, phenomena like category clustering and subjective organization had already pointed to other difficulties for any theory dealing with verbal materials as discrete units (Tulving, 1962).

Finally, formal information theory, which had never been accepted with much enthusiasm by psychologists in the field of learning, had led some investigators to think in these terms long enough to carry out a few very significant investigations. Egger and Miller (1962), for example, showed that secondary reinforcing power acquired by a stimulus depended upon the information value that stimulus had had during previous training with respect to the occurrence or nonoccurrence of a primary reinforcer. In their experiment, rats were presented with compounds of two stimuli. For some subjects, one of these stimuli was redundant; that is, it added nothing to the information carried by the other stimulus about the occurrence or nonoccurrence of a reinforcer. For other subjects, it did provide such information. In tests where the rats were rewarded secondarily for bar pressing, it was clear that the stimulus that had previously been informative was a more effective secondary reinforcer. This demonstration paved the way for the recognition that the key word to use in describing essential conditions for learning is contingency rather than contiguity.

## Contingency Versus Contiguity

Sometimes fundamentally important changes in outlook in our field depend upon developments that seem pretty trivial to students. The statement that one of the necessary conditions for learning is a contingent rather than a contiguous relationship between CS and US in the classical case, and between response and reinforcement in the operant case, is a recent example. Actually the distinction has far-reaching consequences in that the concept of contingency puts the learner in a much more active role in an experiment than the concept of contiguity does. Some of the most interesting recent work in the field of learning is an exploration of those consequences.

The thinking behind this research involves a bit more than simply the idea that contingencies rather than contiguities are essential to learning. Contingencies are treated as variable quantities, and different types of contingencies are considered for the classical and the operant experiments. The definition of a contingency involves two probabilities. In classical conditioning the two probabilities are (a) the probability that the US will be presented given that the CS has been presented [p(US/CS)], and (b) the probability that the US will be presented given that the CS has *not* been presented [p(US/$\overline{CS}$)]. Parallel expressions in operant conditioning are for the probabilities of reinforcement, given that a specified response has or has not occurred: p(RF/R) and p(RF/$\overline{R}$).

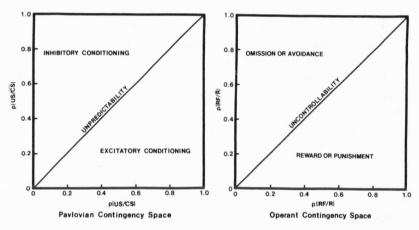

**Figure 4.** Pavlovian (classical) and operant (instrumental) contingency spaces (p = probability; US = unconditioned stimulus; CS = conditioned stimulus; RF = reinforcement; R = response).

In any classical or operant experiment the two relevant contingencies both have meaningful values between .0 and 1.0, and their possible combinations can be located in a *contingency space* (see Figure 4). This graphic representation can provide the basis for several important points. First, the contingency space defines a population of experiments that would be required to spell out the influences of all the various combinations of contingencies. Most of them have not been done. The horizontal axis in either graph in Figure 4 includes the points that represent the various intermittent reinforcement experiments, many of which have been performed. The top of the vertical axis in the graph for the operant case represents the DRO (differential reinforcement of other behavior) schedule, in which reinforcement never occurs following a specific response but does occur in the absence of that response. Such experiments have also been done, but with one exception we know very little about the effects produced by the combinations of contingencies in most of the rest of these spaces.

The one exception is the combinations on the 45° diagonal, which have been studied fairly extensively because they have a special significance. These are the cases where the probability of the US or the reinforcement is identical whether or not the CS or the response of interest has occurred. In the classical case the US is *unpredictable*. This is Rescorla's (1967) truly random control condition for Pavlovian conditioning. In the operant case reinforcement is *uncontrollable*.

An important side point to make here is that the conditions just described are actual, physical, or operational unpredictability and lack of control. The individual subjected to these contingencies may or may not treat them that way. Implicit in this example is one of the most difficult distinctions for students to make, and even an occasional psychologist seems to have trouble with it. Physical lack of control is one thing; the experience of helplessness is something else. It is important to understand that the physical conditions do not guarantee the psychological reaction. Some of the most interesting contingency-based research is on the question of how subjects perceive contingencies and then deal with them.

*Learned Helplessness in Lower Animals*

Before we turn to such matters, I would like to present a summary of current views of learned helplessness, one of the most important lines of research growing out of the contingency analysis. As Maier and Seligman (1976) say in their comprehensive review of these materials,

> There is a simple and elegant experimental design which isolates the effects of controllability from the effects of the outcome being controlled. In this "triadic" design, three groups are used: one group receives as its pretreatment an outcome that it can control by some response. A second group is "yoked"—it receives *exactly* the same physical outcome as its counterpart in the first group, but there is no response the yoked subject can make

which modifies these outcomes. A third group receives no pre-treatment. Later all groups are tested on a new task. . . .

Seligman and Maier (1967) used three groups of 8 dogs. An escape group was trained in a hammock to turn off shock by pressing a panel with its nose. A yoked [control] group received shocks identical in number, duration, and pattern to the shocks delivered to the escape group. . . . A naive control group received no shock in the hammock.

[Twenty-four hours later] all three groups received escape/avoidance training in a shuttle box. . . . The escape group and the naive control group performed well in the shuttle box . . . the yoked control group was considerably slower. . . . Six of the eight subjects in the yoked group failed completely to escape shock. So it was *not the shock itself*, but the inability to control the shock that produced [the helpless] failure to respond.

Maier and Seligman cite a considerable amount of research with dogs, cats, fish, and rats to demonstrate that lack of control over aversive events leads to helplessness and failure to learn in later situations where control is possible. They describe analogous experiments with human subjects that seem to make the same point. Then they go on to argue that experience with uncontrollable events produces deficits that are partly motivational, partly cognitive, and partly emotional. The subject loses the desire (motivation) to respond in an aversive situation, develops the (cognitive) inability to see that control is possible when it becomes possible, and may become anxious and depressed or show other (emotional) disturbances. As this interpretation shows, the concept of learned helplessness has now been extended to include important human psychopathological reactions.

*Extension to Human Behavior*

The reference experiment on learned helplessness in human beings is that of Hiroto (1974). He used the triadic design with college students. One group of subjects, an escape group, learned to turn off an unpleasant loud noise by pushing a button. A yoked group received the same noise, but it occurred independently of their responding. A third group received no noise. After this preliminary experiment all three groups were tested in a hand shuttle box where all they had to do to escape noise was to move the hand from one side to the other. The escape group and the no-noise group performed quite well and quickly learned to shuttle with their hands. In contrast, most of the subjects in the group trained previously with inescapable noise just sat there and passively accepted the unpleasant noise. By including even the type of test employed in the second part of the Seligman and Maier experiment, Hiroto's experiment was a faithful replication, with human subjects, of the studies with lower animals, and the results were much the same.

All of this is very exciting, and even more exciting has been the proposal that the experience of helplessness is a component reaction of depression (Seligman, 1975). Unfortunately, however, there are difficult unresolved problems in this area, and my own judgment is that it is not yet time to tell beginning students that we have available an easy experimental analogue to the development of human helplessness, much less a connection between these laboratory studies and depression. Roth (1980) has recently pointed out some of the difficulties (see also, Abramson, Seligman, & Teasdale, 1978). She treats the production of learned helplessness by noncontingency as a three-stage process:

1. Objective noncontingency → perception of no control.
2. Perception of no control → expectation of future no control.
3. Expectation of no control → learned helplessness.

Looked at this way it at once becomes obvious that there could be many circumstances in which drawing the connecting arrow would be hard to justify. For example, students are frequently not very good at assessing contingencies. In particular, they are bad at detecting the absence of a contingency. All of our efforts in educating our students have gone toward creating an expectation of order, predictability, and control. The fact that these features might be lacking in a situation— even in a psychological experiment—may never dawn on a subject. So far as the connection between learned helplessness and depression is concerned, Alloy and Abramson (1979) have recently come up with an awkward fact related to the perception of contingencies by depressed and nondepressed students. To quote Alloy and Abramson:

> Depressed students' judgments of contingency were surprisingly accurate. . . . Nondepressed students, on the other hand, overestimated the degree of contingency between their responses and outcomes when noncontingent outcomes were frequent and/or desired and underestimated the degree of contingency when contingent outcomes were undesired. (p. 441)

As happens so frequently in our field, the details of the data reveal between-individual and within-individual differences that influence relationships at this initial level in the chain of events leading to learned helplessness. We can expect them to crop up at other levels as well.

Whether the perception of noncontingency leads to the expectation of future noncontingencies seems most likely to depend on the similarity between the situation in which noncontingency is perceived and that in which the expectancy is tested. Most people subjected to uncontrollable noise in a laboratory experiment would not generalize the fact of uncontrollability to everything. But individual differences enter the picture once more. Studies comparing subjects classified as having external or internal locus of control have shown that situational changes that free internals from learned helplessness still produce deficits in external-locus-of-control individuals.

Finally, regarding the question of whether expectancies of no control will lead to learned helplessness, two of the effects of uncontrollability mentioned by Maier and Seligman are probably important: lowered motivation and diminished cognitive ability. It seems likely that the two factors are of very different importance in different treatments of subjects. The complexities just reviewed are enough to urge caution in the claims one makes for the generality of our understanding of the learned helplessness phenomenon.

## Acquisition

The June 6, 1980 issue of *Science* carried a report by Ericsson, Chase, and Faloon that caused a bit of a stir in the international press. I was in England when the report appeared and learned about it first in a substantial (and accurate) account in the *London Times*. This report describes a training program designed to increase the memory span of an undergraduate student, S. F., whose initials are the same as those of the third author of the report. Over two years the student had been provided with more than 230 hours of practice in which random digits were presented at the rate of 1 per second. The subject listened and then attempted to recall the series. If he got them right the next sequence was one digit longer; if he failed to get them right the next series was one digit shorter. At the time of the report in

*Science*, S. F.'s digit span, which initially was 7 items long (as it should be), had increased to almost 80 items, and further practice provided since the report in *Science* has improved S. F.'s memory span to slightly over 80 digits. These spectacular results are plotted in Figure 5.

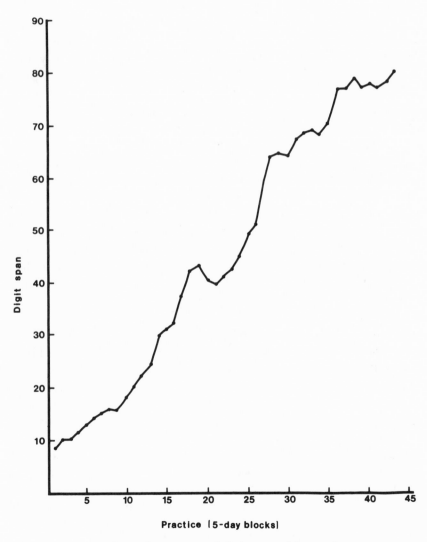

**Figure 5.** Increase of digit span with practice.

In additon to showing an impressive improvement in performance, the details of the data are informative in other ways. Immediately after half of the trials, S. F. reported on his thoughts during the
preceding trial. These reports showed that a part of what S. F. did to
increase his memory span was to use a combination of *chunking* and a
particular *mnemonic device*. He recoded the digits into groups of three
or four digits and gave each grouping an interpretation in terms of
something he knew very well, running times for various races. Thus
"3492 was recoded as '3 minutes and 49 point 2 seconds,' near world-
record mile time!" Later on he supplemented these associations with
others based on ages and dates. More specifically, S. F.'s strategy was
to recode the first part of the list into groups of three and four digits,
leaving a few unrecoded digits to be recalled directly out of short-term
memory. Thus, after about 10 units of practice he could recall 18
digits by recoding 12 of them into three groups of four digits each and
holding the last 6 digits in his rehearsal buffer.

Note that the achievement of this performance followed a plateau in the acquisition function. It was during this period that S. F.
mastered the strategy just described. His second plateau, at about
practice unit 20, occurred when S. F. developed a new hierarchical
strategy. His current retrieval organization can be described as a hierarchy with three levels, and his retrieval structure for 80 digits is illustrated in Figure 6. In Figure 6 the numbers are chunks (except in the
case of items in the rehearsal buffer), the materials in parentheses are
groups of chunks, and the brackets define supergroups.[1]

Probably the first thing to say about these results is that they represent a clear vindication of the ideas of Bryan and Harter (1897),
which have since been rejected because of difficulties of obtaining the
required results in the laboratory. In this experiment we see that
learning takes place in stages separated by plateaus in which new organizations of the materials are achieved. Bryan and Harter reported
that their telegraph operator moved from letter habits to word habits
to sentence habits and that the plateaus occurred when he was developing the skill to move from one level of organization to the next
higher level. S. F.'s performance reveals exactly the same hierarchy of
habits for numbers.

The second thing to say about these data is that they illustrate one

[1] The authors prefer a different terminology. They call the three groups—from
lowest to highest in the hierarchy—*digits, groups,* and *supergroups.*

| LEVEL | NUMBER OF DIGITS | TOTAL |
|---|---|---|
| 1 Supergroups | [(444)(444)][(333)(333)] | |
| | (6×4) + (6×3) | 42 |
| 2 Groups of Chunks | (444) (333) (444) | |
| | (3×4)+(3×3)+(3×4) | 33 |
| 3 Rehearsal Buffer | 5 | 5 |
| | | 80 |

**Figure 6.** S.F.'s retrieval structure for 80 items.

type of interaction between prior knowledge and learning or, in currently popular terminology, between *semantic* and *episodic memory*. S. F. made use of familiar materials—running times—as a sort of semantic crutch to aid in learning. S. F.'s performance when the materials could not be treated as running times showed that his memory deteriorated markedly. Another way to put it is that semantic factors seem to have put constraints on S. F.'s learning just as biological factors do in the case of the animal studies described earlier.

Third, it should be noted that S. F.'s basic memory span did not improve much in this experiment. It was just that what defined an item changed. The organization in Figure 6 represents *at most* a span of 10 items: 5 individual digits in the rehearsal buffer, 3 groups of chunks and 2 supergroups. If the digits in the rehearsal buffer were in two chunks, S. F.'s memory span is still seven, what it was when the experiment began.

Finally, these data point to questions that are of great current interest. Looking again at the graph of S. F.'s performance (Figure 5), we note that the function has increased steadily, except for the occasional plateaus where S. F. achieved new organizations. Going by S. F.'s previous accomplishments, we must ask, "What are the limits that S. F. might reach with further practice? Is there a limit?" A more specific question that will also have occurred to many of you involves the groupings of materials: "Are they becoming 'numerical words' automatically experienced as units out of which the components can be read, just as we automatically see words as units but can report the letters if we are asked to? Are we finally in a position to deal with automatic versus effortful processing?" The recent literature has something to say on both of these questions. Let us begin with the one about the limits of processing capacity.

## Limited Versus Unlimited Capacity

There is plenty of evidence to indicate that under many circumstances, processing capacity is limited and that to devote any of it to a given task is to make less of it available for other purposes. A study reported at the 1979 meeting of the North Carolina Cognitive Group by Britton is a particularly clean example. This experiment involved three groups of individuals who were asked to divide their attention between two tasks and two control groups who performed only one task or the other. The two tasks were (a) reading a passage of printed material for memory and understanding, and (b) responding as rapidly as possible to a click that occurred occasionally. The three experimental groups were asked to devote 10%, 50%, or 90% of their attention to the reading and, thus, 90%, 50%, or 10% of their attention to the click. One of the two other groups devoted 100% of its attention to the reading; no clicks were presented. The other group devoted 100% of its attention to the clicks and did no reading. At the end of the experiment Britton gave a multiple-choice test for recall of what had been read. Thus two measures—percentage correct on the multiple-choice test and reaction time in thousandths of a second—were available, although there was no multiple-choice test for the subjects who did no reading and there were no reaction time data for those who heard no clicks.

The results of the experiment appear in Figure 7, where the total area in the five boxes represents a theoretical total processing capacity and the individual boxes are divided into sections to show how the subjects were instructed to deploy this capacity. The column to the left presents the mean score on the retention test for the four conditions in which those data were available. The column on the right presents mean reaction times for the four conditions in which those data were available. Possibly as remarkable as anything about these results is the indicated effectiveness of the instruction to divide attention in a certain way. It does not seem automatically obvious that people should be able to do so. Beyond that, however, there is clear evidence that devoting a fraction of attention to one task reduces the processing capacity available for the second task.

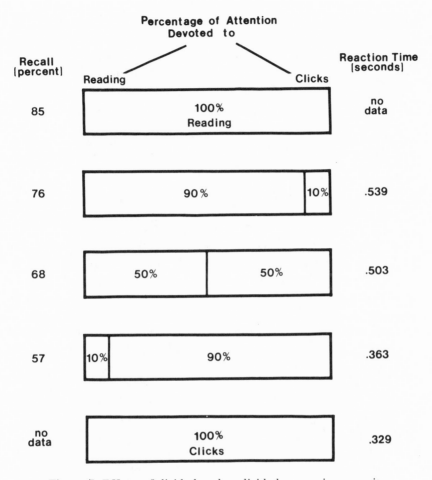

**Figure 7.** Effects of divided and undivided processing capacity.

*Automatic versus effortful processing.* Reading for understanding and reacting as quickly as possible to clicks, as in the experiment just described, require close attention. It seems likely, however, that some materials are processed without such effort. Probably every student has had the experience of remembering the place on a page in a textbook where a forgotten piece of information appeared, of remembering that the lost material was presented early in the professor's lecture last Friday, and of realizing that the piece of information really should be recalled because the professor mentioned it four or five times during the term. Such observations indicate that spatial, temporal, and frequency knowledge may be acquired without special effort or attention.

Discussing this general point, Hasher and Zacks (1979) propose that the processing of spatial, temporal, and frequency information occupy one end of a continuum extending from automatic to effortful processing. The activation of the meaning of a simple word is also near the automatic end of the dimension, an interesting point that I will return to later. The creation of images, rehearsal, organization, and the use of mnemonic devices are toward the effortful end. In between there are other skills, and it seems probable that different specific versions of any skill occupy regions rather than discrete points on the continuum.

The functional characteristics of automatic and effortful processing are still under investigation. Speaking somewhat tentatively for this reason, Hasher and Zacks propose that automatic processes may have the following attributes and effortful processes the opposite ones:

1. Automatic processes occur without intention.

2. They take place without attention, although, if necessary, attention can be directed toward them.

3. They do not interfere with other activities.

4. Once started they tend to run to completion and are hard to inhibit or interrupt. That is, they are not easily interfered with.

5. Some are inherent in the structure of the organism, but some are the result of long practice. It is this final characteristic that justifies the coverage of these particular aspects of information processing in a treatment of learning. Apparently one of the most significant features of information processing is acquired. For example, this must be how the automatic processing of the meanings of words comes about.

*Significance.* The existence of automatic processing is of great adaptive benefit but now and then is also a source of danger. The great adaptive benefit is that automatic processing frees our limited processing capacity for tasks that demand effortful attention. Experienced drivers, for example, put their automobiles on automatic pilot, so to speak, while they drive to work in the morning, devoting their effortful processing devices to making plans for the day—and every now and then they fail to react to an emergency. Accidents caused in this way illustrate the danger of automatic processing alluded to earlier.

A parallel state of affairs exists with respect to listening and reading. There is good reason to believe that both the spoken and the written word are processed automatically. In dichotic-listening experiments the utterance delivered to the unattended ear is forgotten in 3–4 seconds. During brief periods while it is available, however, the meaning registers, presumably automatically, because the listener is concentrating on another message delivered to the other ear. Even more impressive is the behavior of people on the Stroop Color-Word Interference Test, which consists of a list of color names printed in colors other than the colors they name. People trying to name the colors of the ink find that it is impossible to ignore the conflicting color names. The meanings of the words emerge automatically and interfere dramatically with attempts to name the incongruent color in which the words are printed.

At first blush the Stroop effect seems contrary to one of the alleged properties of automatic processes, that they do not interfere with other processes. Presumably those who accept the automatic–effortful distinction would have to hold that the automatic activation of color names and color information is not the locus of interference. Rather, it is the effortful process of pronouncing the color names rather than the color of the ink that creates the difficulty.

*Fixed versus expandable capacity.* Although nothing actually requires them to do so, psychologists interested in the phenomena of automatic processing usually think in terms that assume fairly strict limits on processing capacity. Then they proceed to the point made above, that automatic processing allows this limited capability to deal with important information. Others—for example, Hirst, Spelke, Reaves, Caharick, and Neisser (1980) and Spelke, Hirst, and Neisser (1976)—reject this interpretation in favor of the idea that processing capacity is infinitely expandable.

In support of this interpretation these investigators present data to show that with extended practice—35 to 50 hours of it—college students can learn to read prose materials and take dictation at the same time. After that amount of practice they read as rapidly and understood as much of what they read while taking dictation as they had before the training in tests where all they did was read. Tests without dictation administered during the experiment confirm this interpretation (see Figure 8).

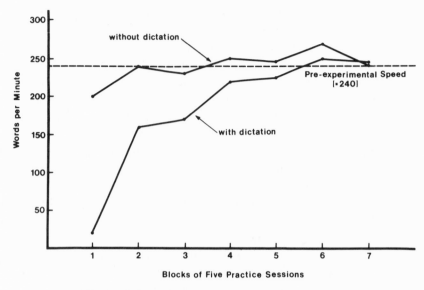

**Figure 8.** Learning to read while taking dictation.

In this experiment some subjects were trained on short stories; others were trained on encyclopedia articles. The results were the same for both. Transfer tests showed that the skill developed with one type of training material generalized to the other. Most impressive of all was the finding in a second experiment that the subjects understood what they took as dictation. In a Bransford and Franks (1971) type of procedure these subjects were tested for the recognition of information that was either a verbatim repetition of something actually dictated, an obvious inference that would be drawn from the dictated material, or an unrelated (usually incorrect) statement. For example, one set of dictated materials were these three sentences:

Cookbooks contain recipes.
Susan owns several.
Mary hates cooking.

The test sentences were these three:

Cookbooks contain recipes (dictated).
Susan owns cookbooks (inference).
Susan hates cooking (unrelated).

The two subjects in the experiment gave confidence ratings based on the degree to which the sentences seemed familiar. The results were that the dictated sentences seemed most familiar, the unrelated sentences seemed least familiar, the inferences fell in between. It is on this basis that Hirst et al. (1980) reject the notion that taking dictation became automatic with practice. The gist of their argument is that

> automatic activities must be relatively simple and routinized. . . . Although *linguistic understanding* is hardly a routine activity, our subjects understood the meanings of sentences and the relations between sentences while simultaneously reading an unrelated story. (p. 106)
>
> In view of this evidence that sentences were understood, it is hard to maintain that they were being handled in an automatic way.
>
> These results strengthen the hypothesis that the ability to divide attention is constrained primarily by the individual's level of skill, not by the size of a fixed pool of resources. (p. 98, italics added)

My own reaction to this interpretation is to question the initial assumption that automatic activities are limited to simple, routinized processing. Or perhaps a better way to put it is that a good many more activities may be simple and routinized than one might suspect. We have already seen that at least one bit of linguistic understanding (see quote above), the meanings of words, is activated automatically. Other evidence obtained by Kintsch and his associates (Baggett, 1975; Keenan & Kintsch, 1974) can be taken to mean that the storage of materials in memory entails an automatic translation of these materials into propositions. As it turns out, the evidence for this assertion also involves inferences. The data indicate quite specifically that 15 or 20 minutes after learning, the truth of a simple inference is as easy for a subject to detect as the truth of a statement actually included in a message, although immediately after learning, the truth of verbatim repetitions can be verified more quickly. Consider these two messages:

> A carelessly discarded burning cigarette started a fire. The fire destroyed many acres of virgin forest.

> A burning cigarette was carelessly discarded. The fire destroyed many acres of virgin forest.

The proposition "the discarded cigarette started the fire" is explicit in the first message, implicit in the second. Immediately after reading one or the other of these versions, subjects recognized the truth of the proposition much more quickly if they had read the version explicitly containing the information. Twenty minutes later, however, they recognized the truth of the proposition equally quickly no matter which proposition they had read. It is hard to believe that the process underlying this performance is anything but automatic in that it does not involve intention, does not require attention, and once started runs to completion. A subject would be most unlikely to arrive at the knowledge that "a burning cigarette was discarded but the fire started some other way."

## Episodic vs. Semantic Memory

One way to put the point of the experiment just described would be to say that immediately after reading, the subjects had a literal *memory* of the message about the cigarette and the fire. Later on they had automatically acquired the *knowledge* that the cigarette started the fire. Another way to put it would be to say that at first the message was in *episodic memory* but that it soon became a part of *semantic memory*. Episodic memory, for each of us, contains a record of temporally dated, autobiographical experience; semantic memory is organized knowledge about the world, including the verbal world of words and conventions for using them (Tulving, 1972; Watkins & Tulving, 1975).

The semantic–episodic distinction has been with us for about a decade, and, predictably, there are those who have turned against it. It is easy to show that the distinction is fuzzy. Most memories have both episodic and semantic elements. Moreover, where understanding is possible, semantic memory seems inevitable given the point just made about the automatic transition of the representation of materials in memory from literal to propositional. In my opinion these points should be taken as observations on the nature of memory rather than as criticisms. Since most memories are an amalgam of episodic and semantic, a major project in the study of learning and memory now becomes that of understanding the relationships between these components. It is already clear that one major relationship is that semantic memory constrains episodic memory just as biological factors constrain other forms of learning. Once again we are back to the main theme identified in the title of this presentation.

*Experimental Empathy*

Let us begin by describing a study that will give us the big picture and then turn to some of the more detailed questions it raises. Anderson and Pichert (1978) had subjects read stories from different perspectives and then attempt to recall the story—sometimes from the perspective in which they originally read the story, sometimes from a different perspective.

> One passage was about two boys playing hooky from school. They go to one of the boys' homes because his mother is never there on Thursdays. The family is well-to-do. They have a fine old home, set back from the road, with attractive grounds. Since it is old it has some defects—a leaky roof, a damp and musty basement. Because the family has considerable wealth, they have a lot of valuable possessions—ten-speed bikes, a color TV set, a rare coin collection. (p. 3)

As a first step in the experiment, the story was broken down into idea units, and raters estimated the importance of the individual elements from three different points of view: that of a prospective burglar, that of a prospective buyer of the home, or no suggested perspective. As the brief passage above shows, some elements, such as the expensive possessions and the fact that no one is home on Thursday, would be important to a burglar. Others, like the leaky roof and spacious grounds, would be important to the prospective purchaser. Finally, separate groups of subjects read the stories and tried to recall them. Some subjects read them from the point of view of a burglar; others read them from the perspective of a homebuyer. Following that, the subjects recalled as much of the story as they could.

Before I describe the outcome of this experiment, let us consider the probable psychological situations of these subjects. The experiment would qualify as an investigation of episodic memory, but different groups are asked to keep certain items from semantic memory in mind as they read and attempt to memorize the story. In one case these items are whatever the subject knows about the habits and preferences of burglars; in the other they include similar information about buying houses. Since the subjects were college students it seems likely that their knowledge of homebuying would be less than their knowledge—from light reading, one trusts—of the burglar's profes-

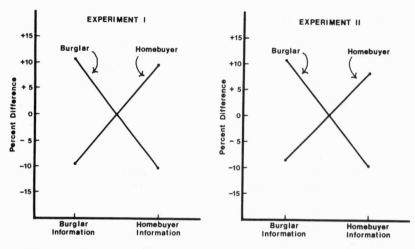

**Figure 9.** In two experiments, what subjects remembered best depended upon the perspective from which they read the material to be remembered.

sion. Certain aspects of the data support such a conclusion. Analysis was confined to 15 items that would be important to a burglar and 15 that would be important to a homebuyer. The student subjects recalled a smaller percentage of the homebuyer material than of the burglar material.

When presented in the most conventional fashion, this feature of the results makes them seem less impressive than they actually are. In order to produce a clear picture of the outcome of the experiment, in Figure 9 I have presented the data as a percentage above or below average for subjects attempting to recall the story from the point of view of a burglar or a homebuyer. The data are broken down into the two sets of items that would be relevant to the interests of one or the other of these individuals. Plotted in this way, the perspective effect is quite impressive. The data indicate that what subjects learned from their reading depended upon the perspective they adopted.

*Encoding Specificity*

That the subjects in this experiment remembered more of the material consonant with the perspective from which they read the story than they did of material consonant with the alternative perspective can be interpreted as a complex application of the encoding specificity principle (Tulving & Thomson, 1973). In its broadest form the principle asserts that we can retrieve only what has been stored and that how it can be retrieved depends upon how it was stored. In a narrower sense the principle implies that the context of storage contains the cues that are required to retrieve the stored item. In an experiment in which a person has to recall a list of words, "the cue *table* facilitates the recall of the target word CHAIR if the original encoding of CHAIR as a to-be-remembered word included semantic information of the kind that defines the relation between two objects in the same conceptual category" (Tulving & Thomson, 1973, p. 359).

In support of this idea, Tulving and Thomson did an experiment in which subjects studied 24 pairs of words like those in Table 1. They were told to learn the capitalized words and that the other word might be of some help in the process. Later on, Tulving and Thomson showed that although their subjects could produce some 60%–70% of the target words when they were provided with the original cue word, they frequently could not even recognize the target word as a target in another context. For example, COLD was usually produced as a response to *ground* but not recognized when paired with *hot*. A part of what makes this impressive is that *ground* and COLD are only weakly associated according to available norms, while the association between *hot* and COLD is a powerful one.

**Table 1**
Cues and Target Words

| Cue | Target word | Cue | Target word |
|---------|-------------|--------|-------------|
| ground | COLD | fruit | FLOWER |
| head | LIGHT | home | SWEET |
| bath | NEED | grasp | BABY |
| cheese | GREEN | butter | SMOOTH |
| stomach | LARGE | drink | SMOKE |
| sun | DAY | beat | PAIN |
| pretty | BLUE | cloth | SHEEP |
| cave | WET | swift | GO |
| whistle | BALL | lady | QUEEN |
| noise | WIND | blade | CUT |
| glue | CHAIR | plant | BUG |
| command | MAN | wish | WASH |

## Levels Versus Elaborateness of Processing

The evidence that encoding is affected by contexts established both by an assumed perspective and by the semantic environment in which a word occurs almost demands that we explore the generality of such effects. In an experiment that I have selected because of the sheer beauty of the data, Fisher and Craik (1977) provide us with one demonstration of generality. They demonstrate the semantic specificity obtained by Tulving and Thomson as well as acoustic specificity and an effect of different *levels of processing*. In their Experiment II, subjects were shown a target word—for example, CAT—together with a cue word that either rhymed (hat-CAT) or was semantically associated (DOG-CAT) with the target. Later on, the subjects were tested, either with the rhyme cue or with the associate. The percentages of target words recalled, shown in Table 2, support the following interpretations:

**Table 2**
Percentage of Words Recalled

| Retrieval cue | Encoding context | | |
|---|---|---|---|
| | Rhyme | Associate | Mean |
| Rhyme | 26 | 17 | 21 |
| Associate | 17 | 44 | 30 |
| Mean | 21 | 30 | — |

1. As the column means show, associative cues were superior to rhyme cues in terms of providing encoding contexts.

2. As the row means show, associative cues were also superior retrieval cues.

3. A comparison of the two diagonals shows encoding specificity for rhymes as well as semantic contexts.

The last of these interpretations suggests that encoding specificity may be an effect with broad generality. Later I will return to the question of how broad. In the meantime, however, please note that the first finding mentioned above, the superiority of semantic over rhyme cues for purposes of encoding, is one of many experimental demonstrations of the importance of the variable called the *level* or *depth* of processing, to which Craik and Lockhart (1972) first called our attention. In this interpretation, semantic and associative activities are "deeper" levels of processing than are reactions to the appearance of a word (Is the word printed in capital letters?) or the sound of a word (Does it rhyme with "hat?"). In the Craik and Lockhart scheme of things, deeper processing is expected to produce better recall, just as happened in the experiment under discussion.

Like most good ideas in our field, the levels-of-processing theory has come in for criticism. More intricate minds than mine have detected circularity when the concept is used for explanatory purposes. It seems to me, since levels can be specified independently of memory, that this criticism is not a sound one, and I shall not pursue the issue further. More important is a criticism which holds that an explanation in terms of levels is incomplete. The data in Table 2 are at least suggestive of the point I wish to make. The existence of encoding specificity for acoustic as well as semantic cues means that both supply possible access routes to the encoded target items. Although these data do not prove it, other evidence (e.g., Goldman & Pellegrino, 1977) shows that multiple codings are more effective than single codes. Thus, if Fisher and Craik had used cues combining rhymes and associations— fat-CAT is the appropriate illustration for the example I used to present the study—memory would have been better than with a single rhyming cue (hat-CAT) or a single semantic cue (dog-CAT). The point is that *in addition to* (I would not accept *instead of*) a concept of levels of processing, a more complete account of encoding mechanisms will have to include a concept of breadth or elaborateness of processing. Evidence in support of this conclusion is abundant (see Craik, 1979).

## *The Durability of Surface Information*

This discussion of acoustic and semantic coding leads to a somewhat tangential point that seems worth making in order to correct a mistaken idea that has had fairly wide circulation recently. It concerns the permanence and importance of semantic as opposed to superficial information in the representation of materials in memory. This idea is that shortly after learning, surface information fades, leaving behind memories that are stored in terms of gists of meaning.

Actually it should have been clear, from the time of Brown and McNeill's (1966) work onward, that this idea could not be correct. Brown and McNeill, you will recall, did a simple but elegant investigation that provided the basic picture of what must be involved in the process of retrieving an item from memory. Retrieval consists of a search through some semantic geographical location in memory for an item with certain prosodic features. The study used students trying to remember a rare word that was "on the tip of their tongues." To remind you of the findings, a student trying to remember that *sextant* is the word defined by the phrase "an instrument for measuring the altitudes of celestial bodies from a moving ship or airplane" reported that the content of consciousness contained a few words associated with the target word: for example, *compass* and *astrolabe*. Most of the information available to the students, however, was more superficial. The subjects were thinking of (and rejecting) words that sounded like the target word. They were also quite accurate in their knowledge of how many syllables the word contained and its initial letter.

All of these findings indicate that surface information must be quite long lasting. The much-cited study of Rubin (1977) supports this point in showing that our longstanding memory for things like Hamlet's soliloquy and the 23rd psalm is verbatim. Similarly, Kintsch and Bates (1977) found substantial verbatim memory two days later for statements included in a classroom lecture. On these bases it seems clear that Bransford and Franks (1971) and certain passages in vintage Kintsch (1974) have made a point that is too extreme. Although the automatic change in the representation of materials in memory from verbatim to gist, as discussed earlier, is surely a real phenomenon, it is important to understand that the conversion is not a total one. Residual surface features are retained and seem to exist partly as a mode of representation and partly to play a role in the process of retrieval.

## State-Dependent Learning

To return now to the main theme of this presentation, one implication of the encoding specificity principle is that the reinstatement of the context of learning favors the recall of what was learned in that context. So far we have looked at that idea only in terms of the context provided by an assumed perspective (burglar or homebuyer) and by the retrieval cues presented along with to-be-remembered target items. There is an abundance of evidence that the influence is a very general one, however. Experimental results dating back at least to the 1950s show that retention is better in the physical environment where learning occurred than elsewhere. There is even evidence that odor cues present at the time of learning can sometimes be powerful reminders of those occasions. To quote Rubin (Note 1),

> The first example, which comes from a paper by Banister and Zangwill (1941), is the report of Dr. E. J. Lindgen, an anthropologist: "I was recently driving Mr. and Mrs. L. from my house into Cambridge when I became gradually aware of the most delightful sensation, and presently identified it as caused by a smell. This seemed so exceptionally overwhelming in its pleasantly drug-like effect that I felt obliged to attend further to it and to try to give it a name. Suddenly it came: 'Mongolia.' . . . it was in fact Mongol tobacco" (p. 173).
>
> The following example comes from a paper by Laird (1935) in which 254 men and women of eminence, averaging 52.5 years old, were asked about odors as revivers of memories. One subject responded: "On the train once, in the midst of happy conditions, I suddenly felt discouraged, awkward, unhappy. As soon as I recognized the perfume used by a fellow traveler, I saw very vividly a large dancing class, a French dancing master, and felt again my girlish dismay at his attitude toward my poor attempts to learn the steps he was trying to teach me" (p. 128).
>
> Similar effects were easily produced [with] a sample of common odors in a pilot study in our laboratory. Consider the following description from a female undergraduate, age 19, who had just smelled an unlabeled bottle containing mothballs: "Musty corners of closets in our cottage in Michigan. I remember finding ancient toys, books, from when my grandfather was little. . . . A treasure chest!" Her age at the time of the remembered event was reported as 10. A 19-year-old male who had just smelled an unlabeled bottle containing peppermint also reported a 9-year-old memory: "Candy Christmas canes at my aunt's house. They were on the tree, just a few left because it was after Christmas."

Finally, there is evidence that learning is state dependent—that is, that the psychological (e.g., emotional) and physiological (e.g., drug) state of the individual at the time of learning constitutes a part of the stimulus context that controls the products of learning. In the latter case, experiments show drug-dependent learning in animals and humans for the drugs in most common use, including marijuana, barbiturates, amphetamines, and alcohol.

Weingartner and his associates (Weingartner, Aderfis, Eich, & Murphy, 1976) had female subjects learn and attempt to recall lists of 10 words under the four conditions produced by a crossing of learning and recall when sober or intoxicated—probably quite intoxicated. To produce this condition the women were served a screwdriver cocktail consisting, on the average, of a triple shot of vodka mixed with six ounces of orange juice. Among the various signs that this was enough to produce intoxication was the fact that when sober, the subjects recalled 58% of the words in the list on an immediate test and when intoxicated, they recalled 42%.

Half of the words to be learned were high-imagery nouns; the other half were low-imagery nouns. This difference had no effect when the subjects were sober: They remembered an identical average of 5.8 high- and low-imagery words. When intoxicated they recalled 4.4 of the high-imagery words and 4.0 of the low-imagery words. The primary data in the experiment were the percentages of these words still retained in the latter test. The data show a drug-dependent effect for both types of words. That is, subjects were able to recall words best in a replication of the state in which they originally learned the words (see Figure 10).

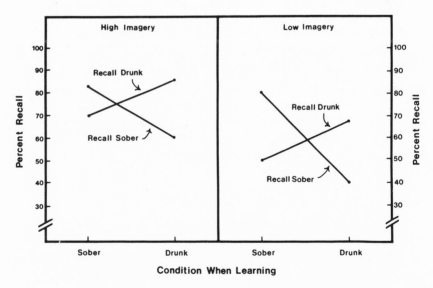

**Figure 10.** State-dependent learning.

## Spheres of Influence

The question of how physiological and psychological states have their effects on learning seems to have two answers: (a) They affect the nature of the materials selected for encoding, and (b) they provide access routes to coded memories. I have already covered some of the evidence for both of these points. The Anderson and Pichert (1978) experiment illustrates the first point; subjects tended to select for encoding material that was congruent with an assumed perspective. The encoding specificity and state-dependent learning material make the second point: Cues and conditions present at the time of learning are useful for purposes of reviving a memory.

It would be comforting if I could tell you that these effects are completely general, but they are not. Experimental data begin to define the sphere of influence in which encoding specificity operates. I shall develop this point by describing some work related to the question of whether learning is mood dependent—that is, whether the reinstatement of the emotional condition that was present at the time of learning is an aid to memory.

In a presentation at the convention of the American Psychological Association for which this paper was prepared, Bower (Note 2) described some fascinating experimental work showing such state dependency. I will attempt to reconstruct the general procedures by describing a less successful experiment that followed. The chief difference between the two was that the work reported earlier (Bower, Note 2) involved lists of fairly discrete items. The follow-up work (Bower, Gilligan, & Monteiro, in press) involved discourse.

The subjects in these experiments were hypnotized, and a sad or happy mood was induced in different individuals. Before coming out of the trance they were given a posthypnotic suggestion to experience the same mood when they were given a passage of materials to read and learn. While they were in this sad or happy frame of mind (having been returned to a normal, waking state),

> all subjects read a 660-word narrative that described four different age-regression sessions involving a male patient (Paul Smith) undergoing hypnotherapy with a psychiatrist. Except for brief setting statements and the framework of beginning and ending the four therapeutic sessions, the narrative mainly depicted Paul recalling and relating a carefully balanced variety of happy,

neutral, and sad incidents from his life. The text was divided into 78 basic idea units (roughly, simple clauses), of which 26 came from descriptions of happy incidents, 26 from sad incidents, and 26 from neutral incidents. Examples of happy items were memories of riding piggy-back on his father's back, jokes he had been told, festive family gatherings, receiving good grades in school, winning a football game, and his first true love. Sad memories included the deaths of his grandfather and his dog, being cut from his baseball squad, the break-up of the Beatles music group, and his sister's injuries in an auto accident. Neutral items usually referred to the setting information, the beginning trance induction or ending trance termination of Paul at each session, remarks between the doctor and Paul about his progress. (Bower, et al., in press)

After reading the story the subjects were returned to the trance state. Again they were provided with a sad or happy mood, but in this stage of the experiment, half of the subjects were returned to the original mood under which they had read the materials to be learned; the other half were put into the alternative mood. The subjects were then given the posthypnotic suggestion to experience upon awakening the mood they were in while hypnotized. Once out of the trance and in either a sad or happy mood, they were asked to recall the story either in the same state as that in which they had read the story or in a different state. The experimental design, as will be seen, was a 2 $\times$ 2 factorial.

The subjects' recall protocols revealed several interesting things. First, in agreement with the Anderson and Pichert experiment with different perspectives, subjects who had read the story when happy remembered more of the happy details. Those who had read the story while sad remembered more of the sad ones. Mood at time of acquisition had led to a selectivity in what was acquired. Mood at the time of recall had no such effect. This result is fairly routine in research of this type: The provision of a theme, category information, or some other information that is useful for encoding is of little value as a retrieval cue. Finally, in this experiment there was no dependable evidence for mood-dependent memory. Subjects actually remembered slightly less when their recall was tested in an affective state different from the one existing at the time of learning than they remembered when recall was tested in the same affective state existing at the time of learning. However, this effect fell far short of statistical significance.

As I mentioned earlier, the chief difference between this study, which failed to show mood-dependent learning, and the studies that did lies in the nature of the materials. Results obtainable with lists of items may not show up with stories or other organized materials. This will come as a reminder to those who have been in touch with the literature on human learning and memory for a while. For those who have not, let me just mention that the positive effects of distributed practice frequently do not work with discourse. The benefits of filling a retention interval with sleep rather than with waking activity some-times disappear with passages of prose. More recently, in a part of the Anderson and Pichert experiment which I have not described, these investigators found that subjects who switched from one perspective to the other were able to recall a few relevant details from the story about the boys playing hooky that they had not remembered in the alternative perspective. Once more it seems important to urge caution when it comes to attributing degrees of generality to experimental data.

## Maintenance of Knowledge

In previous sections I have described some materials related to the process of getting information into memory (learning) and others re-lated to getting it back out again (retrieval). I would like next to touch briefly on a neglected problem in our field, the problem of keeping materials in memory once they are there. The problem is a neglected one, I suspect, because of the "relatively permanent" clause that is a part of most definitions of learning, as well as the belief in some quar-ters that "relatively permanent" actually means "absolutely perma-nent." These views may be correct for laboratory learning, sur-rounded as it is by a protective fence to keep out interference. But as anyone can tell you who has ever had a delayed test, in real life, of recall for anything after a period away from the material, the concept of permanent memory is mythological. As a part of his study of very long-term biographical memories, Bahrick (1979) did some studies that lead to interesting ideas in this area. He studied the most obvious candidate for inclusion in the list of variables that might keep memo-ries intact—rehearsal—but his first experiments already had added to our understanding of the role of practice in the maintenance of memory.

In one experiment on this topic, Bahrick allowed subjects to re-hearse English–Spanish vocabulary items under different distributions of practice. The subjects first learned the vocabulary to a criterion of one correct recitation by the *drop-out method,* in which, on trials following the first trial, only the items missed on the just-previous trial were presented. Next, subjects received five rehearsal trials using the same procedure, but three different groups received them at different temporal spacings. In terms of days between sessions, the intervals were 0 (sessions all came on the same day, one immediately after the other), 1 day, and 30 days. Finally, all subjects were tested 30 days after the last session.

The data (see Figure 11) show several interesting things. Acquisition was most rapid under the massed-practice condition. Greater separation produced slower learning. Presumably this is because there is a loss of learning between sessions: The longer the intersession interval, the greater the loss. In every practice condition, however, there was a net saving, so that improvement occurred in all of them. The tests after 30 days show an interesting effect: Recall was best for the subjects whose intersession interval had been 30 days and whose performance up to then had been somewhat inferior. Bahrick believes this means that subjects practicing with shorter intersession intervals had not learned the rehearsal techniques required for long-term retention.

These results also prompted Bahrick to ask an interesting practical question: If one wanted to keep a person's knowledge of the Spanish vocabulary permanently up to the high level achieved by the zero and one-day groups, what kind of rehearsal program would be required? Would it be best to have a series of intensive practice sessions separated by long periods of time, shorter practice sessions more frequently, or what? Bahrick's answer is that there would be a family of *trade-off functions*—combinations of temporal separations and amounts of practice—that would keep this knowledge intact. Small amounts of rehearsal would have to be frequent; large amounts of rehearsal could be less often.

To provide data to analyze for the purpose of estimating these trading relations, Bahrick determined the memory for street names and street sequences in Delaware, Ohio, for alumni of Ohio Wesleyan University located in that city. The subjects had graduated at times prior to the experiment ranging from a little over 1 year to a little over

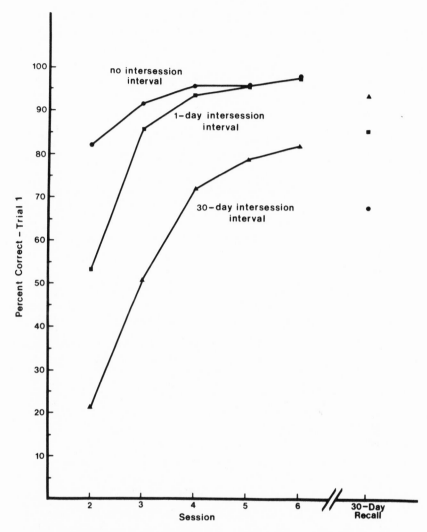

**Figure 11.** Effects of three different distributions of practice upon learning and 30-day retention.

46 years. In the interim they had visited Delaware various numbers of times for various lengths of time. The visits also varied in recency and temporal pattern. Bahrick used a regression analysis of these data to obtain the desired estimates. A portion of the data, presented in Figure 12, answers a very specific question: "If a person comes to Delaware for 1-, 2-, 3-, 4-, or 5-day visits a number of times a year and is

tested for memory for street names a month after the last visit, how many visits and how many total days per year would be required to keep this memory at the level a student had at the time of graduation?" As you can see, short visits would have to be more numerous but would be the most efficient in terms of the total time required.

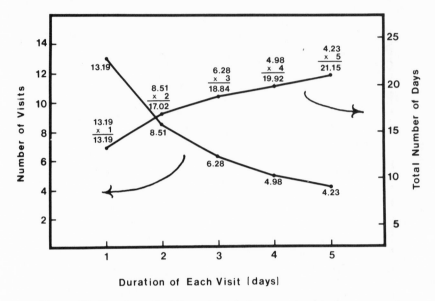

**Figure 12.** Number of visits and total time required to keep a memory intact as a function of the duration of visits.

## Conclusion

As your guide on this rambling trip through the domain of learning I have tried, in the space available, to call your attention to the highlights, some of which you may want to return to and explore further on your own. If you do you will find that the papers I have cited usually contain a background discussion that will head you in the right direction. You will also find, as I did in planning our itinerary, that the province of learning is criss-crossed with a network of side roads and country lanes. Many of them are inviting, but some of them have no exits and others are private toll roads where the fees are collected by the only inhabitant of a remote and lonely territory. Some of them, I suspect, are included in other tours conducted by other leaders of our organization. If you have not signed on for any of these journeys, or if you want to make the visits on your own, I believe that you might profit from an acquaintance with (a) the new economic models of behavior that provide impressive accounts of how animals allocate their energies to various activities (Staddon, 1980), (b) developments in the study of biofeedback and its place in the burgeoning field of behavioral medicine (Miller, 1978), and (c) concept attainment treated in terms of the hypotheses adopted by the learner (Phillips & Levine, 1975). Or you may just want to consult the guidebooks to refresh your acquaintance with the general territory. If so, the books that I have found most useful are those of Schwartz (1978) on conditioning and animal learning and Kintsch (1977) on human learning and memory. Whatever your tour plans, bon voyage!

### Reference Note

1. Rubin, D. Personal communication, July 28, 1980.
2. Bower, G. *Emotional mood and memory.* Paper presented at the meeting of the American Psychological Association, Montreal, Quebec, Canada, September 3, 1980.

### References

Abramson, L. Y., Seligman, M. E. P., & Teasdale, J. D. Learned helplessness in humans: Critique and reformulation. *Journal of Abnormal Psychology,* 1978, *87,* 49–74.

Alloy, L. B., & Abramson, L. Y. Judgment of contingency in depressed and nondepressed students. *Journal of Experimental Psychology: General,* 1979, *108,* 441–485.

Amsel, A. Partial reinforcement effects on vigor and persistence. In K. W. Spence & J. T. Spence (Eds.), *The psychology of learning and motivation* (Vol. 1). New York: Academic Press, 1967.

Anderson, R. C., & Pichert, J. W. Recall of previously unrecallable information following a shift in perspective. *Journal of Verbal Learning and Verbal Behavior,* 1978, 17, 1–12.

Baggett, P. Memory for explicit and implicit information in picture stories. *Journal of Verbal Learning and Verbal Behavior,* 1975, *14,* 538–548.

Bahrick, H. P. Maintenance of knowledge: Questions about memory we forgot to ask. *Journal of Experimental Psychology: General,* 1979, *108,* 296–308.

Banister, H., & Zangwill, O. L. Experimentally induced olfactory paramnesias. *British Journal of Psychology,* 1941, *32,* 155–175.

Bolles, R. C. Species-specific defense reactions and avoidance learning. *Psychological Review,* 1970, 77, 32–48.

Bower, G. H., Gilligan, S. G., & Monteiro, K. P. Selective learning caused by affective states. *Journal of Experimental Psychology: General,* in press.

Bransford, J. D., & Franks, J. J. The abstraction of linguistic ideas. *Cognitive Psychology,* 1971, *2,* 330–350.

Breland, K., & Breland, M. The misbehavior of organisms. *American Psychologist,* 1961, *16,* 681–684.

Brown, P., & Jenkins, H. M. Autoshaping of the pigeon's keypeck. *Journal of the Experimental Analysis of Behavior*, 1968, *11*, 1–8.

Brown, R., & McNeill, D. The "tip of the tongue" phenomenon. *Journal of Verbal Learning and Verbal Behavior*, 1966, *5*, 325–337.

Bryan, W. L., & Harter, N. Studies in the physiology and the psychology of the telegraphic language. *Psychological Review*, 1897, *7*, 345–375.

Craik, F. I. M. Human memory. *Annual Review of Psychology*, 1979, *30*, 63–102.

Craik, F. I. M., & Lockhart, R. S. Levels of processing: A framework for memory research. *Journal of Verbal Learning and Verbal Behavior*, 1972, *11*, 671–684.

Egger, M. D., & Miller, N. E. Secondary reinforcement in rats as a function of information value and reliability of the stimulus. *Journal of Experimental Psychology*, 1962, *64*, 97–104.

Ericsson, K. A., Chase, W. G., & Faloon, S. Acquisition of a memory skill. *Science*, 1980, *208*, 1181–1182.

Fisher, R. P., & Craik, F. I. M. Interaction between encoding and retrieval operations in cued recall. *Journal of Experimental Psychology: Human Learning and Memory*, 1977, *3*, 701–711.

Garcia, J., & Koelling, R. A. The relation of cue to consequence in avoidance learning. *Psychonomic Science*, 1966, *4*, 123–124.

Garcia, J., & Rusiniak, K. W. What the nose learns from the mouth. In D. Müller-Schwartze & R. M. Silverstein (Eds.), *Chemical signals*. New York: Plenum, 1980.

Goldman, S. R., & Pellegrino, J. W. Processing domain, encoding elaboration, and memory trace strength. *Journal of Verbal Learning and Verbal Behavior*, 1977, *16*, 29–43.

Grant, D. A. Adding communication to the signaling property of the CS in classical conditioning. *Journal of General Psychology*, 1968, *79*, 147–175.

Grice, G. R., & Hunter, J. J. Stimulus intensity effects depend upon the type of experimental design. *Psychological Review*, 1964, *71*, 247–256.

Guthrie, E. R., & Horton, G. P. *Cats in a puzzle box*. New York: Rinehart, 1946.

Hasher, L., & Zacks, R. T. Automatic and effortful processing in memory. *Journal of Experimental Psychology: General*, 1979, *108*, 356–388.

Hiroto, D. S. Locus of control and learned helplessness. *Journal of Experimental Psychology*, 1974, *102*, 187–193.

Hirst, W., Spelke, E. S., Reaves, C. C., Caharick, G., & Neisser, U. Dividing attention without alternation or automaticity. *Journal of Experimental Psychology: General*, 1980, *109*, 98–117.

Keenan, J. M., & Kintsch, W. The identification of explicitly and implicitly presented information. In W. Kintsch, *The representation of meaning in memory*. Hillside, N.J.: Erlbaum, 1974.

Kendler, H. H., & Kendler, T. S. Mediation and conceptual behavior. In K. W. Spence & J. T. Spence (Eds.), *The psychology of learning and motivation* (Vol. 2). New York: Academic Press, 1968.

Kimble, G. A. *Principles of general psychology* (1st ed.). New York: Ronald Press, 1956.

Kimble, G. A. Attitudinal factors in eyelid conditioning. In G. A. Kimble (Ed.), *Foundations of conditioning and learning*. New York: Appleton-Century-Crofts, 1967.

Kimble, G. A., & Garmezy, N. *Principles of general psychology* (3rd ed.). New York: Ronald Press, 1968.

Kimble, G. A., Garmezy, N., & Zigler, E. *Principles of general psychology* (5th ed.). New York: Wiley, 1980.

Kimble, G. A., & Perlmuter, L. C. The problem of volition. *Psychological Review*, 1970, *77*, 361–384.

Kintsch, W. *The representation of meaning in memory.* Hillside, N.J.: Erlbaum, 1974.

Kintsch, W. *Memory and cognition* (2nd ed.). New York: Wiley, 1977.

Kintsch, W., & Bates, E. Recognition memory for statements from a classroom lecture. *Journal of Experimental Psychology: Human Learning and Memory,* 1977, *3,* 150–159.

Laird, P. A. What can you do with your nose? *Scientific Monthly,* 1935, *41,* 126–130.

Lenneberg, E. H. On explaining language. In M. E. P. Seligman & J. L. Hager (Eds.), *Biological boundaries of learning.* New York: Appleton-Century-Crofts, 1972.

Maier, S. F., & Seligman, M. E. P. Learned helplessness: Theory and evidence. *Journal of Experimental Psychology: General,* 1976, *105,* 3–46.

McGovern, J. B. Extinction of associations in four transfer paradigms. *Psychological Monographs,* 1964, *78,* (Whole No. 593).

Miller, N. E. Theory and experiment relating psychoanalytic displacement to stimulus–response generalization. *Journal of Abnormal and Social Psychology,* 1948, *43,* 155–178.

Miller, N. E. Biofeedback and visceral learning. *Annual Review of Psychology,* 1978, *29,* 373–404.

Moore, B. R., & Stuttard, S. Dr. Guthrie and *Felis domesticus* Or: Tripping over the cat. *Science,* 1979, *205,* 1031–1033.

Öhman, A., Fredrikson, M., Hugdahl, K., & Rimmö, P. The premise of equipotentiality in human classical conditioning: Conditioned electrodermal responses to potentially phobic stimuli. *Journal of Experimental Psychology: General,* 1976, *105,* 313–337.

Pavlov, I. P. *Conditioned reflexes.* Oxford, England: Oxford University Press, 1927.

Phillips, S., & Levine, M. Probing for hypotheses with adults and children: Blank trials and introtacts. *Journal of Experimental Psychology: General,* 1975, *104,* 327–354.

Postman, L., & Stark, K. The role of response availability in transfer and interference. *Journal of Experimental Psychology,* 1969, *79,* 168–177.

Rescorla, R. A. Pavlovian conditioning and its proper control procedures. *Psychological Review,* 1967, *74,* 71–80.

Rescorla, R. A., & LoLordo, V. M. Inhibition of avoidance behavior. *Journal of Comparative and Physiological Psychology,* 1965, *59,* 406–412.

Revusky, S., & Garcia, J. Learned associations over long delays. In G. Bower (Ed.), *The psychology of learning and motivation: Advances in research and theory* (Vol. 4). New York: Academic Press, 1970.

Roth, S. A revised model of learned helplessness in humans. *Journal of Personality,* 1980, *48,* 103–133.

Rubin, D. C. Very long term memory for prose and verse. *Journal of Verbal Learning and Verbal Behavior,* 1977, *16,* 611–621.

Rumbaugh, D. M., & Savage-Rumbaugh, E. S. A response to Herbert Terrace's paper, *Linguistic Apes. Psychological Record,* 1980, *30,* 315–318.

Samelson, F. J. B. Watson's Little Albert, Cyril Burt's twins, and the need for a critical science. *American Psychologist,* 1980, *35,* 619–625.

Schwartz, B. *Psychology of learning and behavior.* New York: W. W. Norton, 1978.

Seligman, M. E. P. *Helplessness—On depression, development, and death.* San Francisco: W. H. Freeman, 1975.

Seligman, M. E. P., & Maier, S. F. Failure to escape traumatic shock. *Journal of Experimental Psychology,* 1967, *74,* 1–9.

Skinner, B. F. "Superstition" in the pigeon. *Journal of Experimental Psychology,* 1948, *38,* 168–172.

Spelke, E. S., Hirst, W. C., & Neisser, U. Skills of divided attention. *Cognition,* 1976, *4,* 215–230.

Spence, K. W. Cognitive factors in the extinction of the conditioned eyeblink in human subjects. *Science*, 1963, *140*, 1224–1225.

Staddon, J. E. R. *Limits to action: The allocation of individual behavior*. New York: Academic Press, 1980.

Staddon, J. E. R., & Simmelhag, V. L. The "superstition" experiment: A reexamination of its implications for the principles of adaptive behavior. *Psychological Review*, 1971, *78*, 3–43.

Terrace, H. S., Pettito, L. A., Sanders, R. J., & Bever, T. G. Can an ape create a sentence? *Science*, 1979, *206*, 891–900.

Tulving, E. Subjective organization in free recall of "unrelated" words. *Psychological Review*, 1962, *69*, 344–354.

Tulving, E. Episodic and semantic memory. In E. Tulving & W. Donaldson (Eds.), *Organization of memory*. New York: Academic Press, 1972.

Tulving, E., & Thomson, D. Encoding specificity and retrieval processes in episodic memory. *Psychological Review*, 1973, *80*, 352–373.

Valentine, C. W. The innate bases of fear. *Journal of Genetic Psychology*, 1930, *37*, 394–419.

Watkins, M. J., & Tulving, E. Episodic memory: When recognition fails. *Journal of Experimental Psychology: General*, 1975, *104*, 5–29.

Watson, J. B., & Rayner, R. Conditioned emotional reactions. *Journal of Experimental Psychology*, 1920, *3*, 1–14.

Weingartner, H., Aderfis, W., Eich, J. E., & Murphy, D. L. Encoding imagery specificity in alcohol state-dependent learning. *Journal of Experimental Psychology: Human Learning and Memory*, 1976, *2*, 83–87.

DAVID ELKIND

# RECENT RESEARCH IN COGNITIVE AND LANGUAGE DEVELOPMENT

**D**avid Elkind, professor and chair of the Eliot-Pearson Department of Child Study at Tufts University, is one of the leading researchers in child development. His publication list contains more than 200 items and includes research studies, review and theoretical articles, book chapters, books, and more popular pieces for magazines. Elkind earned his doctorate in clinical psychology at the University of California, Los Angeles in 1955 and spent the next year as a postdoctoral fellow with David Rapaport at the Austen Riggs Center. In 1964–65 he spent a year at Piaget's Centre D'Epistemologie Genetique in Geneva. Before coming to Tufts he spent 12 years at the University of Rochester as professor of psychology, psychiatry, and education.

Elkind's research has focused on cognitive and perceptual development, areas in which he has attempted to build upon the research of Jean Piaget. His most recent books include *Child Development and Education: A Piagetian Perspective,* (1976); *Human Development: Contemporary Perspectives* (with D. Hetzel, 1977); *Development of the Child* (with I. Weiner, 1978); *The Child's Reality: Three Developmental Themes* (1978); and *The Child and Society: Essays in Applied Child Development* (1979).

Elkind is consulting editor to many psychological journals, is a member of some 10 professional organizations, and is a consultant to government agencies, state education departments, clinics, and mental health centers. He also lectures extensively in the United States and Canada.

In this paper, Elkind draws on the most recent literature in a variety of related areas to describe the major contemporary trends in developmental studies of language and thought.

DAVID ELKIND

# RECENT RESEARCH IN COGNITIVE AND LANGUAGE DEVELOPMENT

**A**ny attempt to survey recent research in the area of cognitive and language development in a brief article has, of necessity, to be selective. Before proceeding further, then, let me share my criteria for selection. First, each area of research reported here constitutes a major trend, an area in which many investigators are working, communicating, and challenging one another. Topics, no matter how interesting or important, that engage the interest of only one or a few investigators are not considered. Second, the trends reported are those that seem to have momentum and to be gaining new followings rather than losing or merely maintaining their hold on investigators' time and energies. Finally, only major problems or issues are reviewed; fine-grained research and analysis of highly technical issues are not covered.

Even with these guidelines, the corpus of studies to be covered is large indeed. There are of necessity omissions of work that some will feel strongly should have been included. I apologize for whatever narrowness or shortsightedness is found in this review. No topics or investigators were intentionally slighted or omitted. My biases, insofar as I am aware of them, are professional and academic rather than personal. If anything major has been omitted, my plea is ignorance, not malice. However, in this case ignorance of the literature is not pleaded as an excuse, but only given as an explanation.

With these preliminaries out of the way, we can move to the major task of the presentation. This review is organized into two sections: recent research in cognition and recent investigations in the area of language.

# Research in Cognition

## Social Cognition

Work in cognitive development continues to be prominent and shows some new directions in both content and theorizing. A growing body of work deals with the new content area of *children's social conceptions.* Furth's (1980) recent work on how children view money and social roles and institutions is a case in point. Other work of this sort is looking into how children conceptualize parents and parenting. It appears that children's concern with maternal autonomy, control, and physical nurturance declines with age. At the same time, the need for psychological nurturance increases with age (Weisz, 1980).

Other work in new content areas includes some interesting investigations of *children's scientific thinking.* As described by Siegler (1978), children first have the ability to acquire existing knowledge, then they are able to encode this knowledge, next they develop the ability to acquire new knowledge, and finally they are able to deal with feedback or continuous information flow in their scientific endeavors. One particularly interesting finding is that five-year-olds use systematic strategies in dealing with science problems.

A couple of other new content areas should be mentioned. Perrin (1981) has done a study of *children's conceptions regarding the causes, prevention, and treatment of illness.* Young children (5–7 years old) recognize illness by external signs, believe sickness results from a concrete action or the lack of it, think they can keep from getting sick by obeying a set of rules, and think that they will recover either automatically or by rigidly adhering to another set of rules.

As children mature, they define illness by concrete symptoms rather than the need to go to bed, and they attribute the cause of illness to germs, which have a powerful, even magical, effect upon the body. Illness can be avoided by staying out of the way of these germs: "Don't go near sick people." Recovery from illness occurs as a result of taking medicine and doing what the doctor says. Adolescent subjects understand illness in all of its complexity. They recognize, for example, that a given symptom like fever can signal different kinds of illness. They also recognize that the same illness can affect different people in different ways. At this age young people also appreciate the complexities of treatment and cure. But even at this age concepts of prevention are still difficult to grasp. Prevention is apparently more difficult to understand than either causation or treatment.

One last new content area is of interest. Behmer and I (Elkind & Behmer, Note 1) have just collected data on *children's conception of the clergy*. We looked at Catholic children's conceptions of priests, Protestant children's conceptions of ministers, and Jewish children's conceptions of rabbis. We looked at what children thought the clergy did, how children thought people came to the clergy, and how children viewed this profession in comparison to other social roles.

The results were comparable for all three groups. Young children saw the clergy in global terms as people associated with the church or synagogue, who got there because they wanted to be there or because someone picked them. They were also seen as working only on the weekends. Older children had a more differentiated conception of the clergy. They thought the clergyperson's job was to lead the service, say prayers, etc. Of particular interest was the fact that children at this stage said that clergy learned their role in a kind of apprenticeship fashion, from someone else. They also recognized the clergy as a profession like other professions. Among the adolescents, the clergy's role was seen in more general, abstract terms. The job was seen as entailing multiple functions (weddings, funerals, etc.), and entrance into the clergy was perceived to be achieved by going to a special training or educational program. Adolescents viewed the occupational role of the clergy as comparable to that of members of other professions such as physicians or lawyers. Perhaps the most striking finding of the study was the secular view children held of the clergy. There was no evidence, in our data, that children viewed priests, rabbis, or ministers as "chosen" or "called" in any particular way. The clergy was seen as a profession very much like any other.

Let me turn now to some process issues on the contemporary scene that are of particular interest. One has to do with *a reconcept-*

*ualization of the Piagetian stages,* a kind of neo-Piagetian approach. Foremost among this work is that of Juan Pascual-Leone (1970). It is not possible to summarize his complex and intricate theory here, but it probably does not do violence to it to say that Pascual-Leone postulates an *"m* space" that constitutes the child's information-processing capacity at any given time. The capacity to deal with more and more elements simultaneously increases with development but is related to many other variables as well. The concept of *m* space provides Pascual-Leone with a flexible and researchable developmental construct. Case (1978), another "neo-Piagetian," builds upon Pascual-Leone's work and adds the concept of automatization as a prime mechanism of moving from one stage to another.

Another current process issue derives from a group of writers whose work deals with *social cognition and moral development*—namely, Kohlberg (1976), Selman (1976), Habermass (1970), and Edelstein, Keller, and Wahlen (Note 2). This issue is the relation of cognitive structures to structures of social cognition. Several possibilities exist. First, it might be that social cognition is simply a matter of applying to the social world cognitive processes utilized in dealing with the physical world. The role-taking literature to be reviewed later appears to have started from this assumption and even used a physical task— Piaget's well-known three-mountains task—as a paradigm.

A second possibility is that some aspects of social cognition are independent of but related to the cognitive operations described by Piaget. Habermass (1974), for example, suggests that certain strategic and communicative actions originate outside the realm of the basic cognitive operations. Finally, Kohlberg (1978) and Selman and Jacquette (1979) appear to be saying that cognitive processes may involve a different system of mental operations than that ascribed to them by Piaget. From this perspective, the operations used in social reasoning and judgment are different in fundamental respects from those employed in reasoning and judgment about the physical world.

Concern with the uniqueness of social cognition fits nicely into work in education that is going on both in Israel and in the United States and that deals with the role of the adult in the child's learning and development. It is probably fair to say that both the humanists and the behaviorists take a Rousseau-like view of the child in the sense that it is the child who must do the learning, whether the child is allowed, in Dewey's terms, to "unfold from within" or is "enforced from without." In contrast, a new perspective is emerging which suggests that the adult is not separate from the child but has to be seen as part of the child's adaptive apparatus.

Perhaps the most extensive work in this domain has been done by Feuerstein (1980) and his colleagues in Israel. Feuerstein speaks of "mediated learning experiences," by which he means that adults, in a way, "predigest" experiences for young people. This predigestive activity can enable children to handle stimuli they could not handle on their own. As a consequence they acquire what I have called (Elkind, Note 3) secondary schemata of adaptation and accommodation for dealing with the world that are social in origin. Schemata of attention, for example, in which past experience is used in making judgments, are largely socially acquired.

Accordingly, the work of Kohlberg (1976), Selman and Jacquette (1977), and Feuerstein (1980), as well as my own (Elkind, in press), does indeed suggest that social cognition involves more than the application of Piagetian operations to social contents. My own hypothesis (Elkind, in press) is that secondary schemata of assimilation and accommodation are "mediating structures" that are acquired by means of reflective abstraction from adults to whom the child is emotionally attached. Piaget proposed reflective abstraction (abstraction from the child's own actions rather than from things) as the origin, in part, of intellectual operations. I am suggesting that children can acquire mediating structures (secondary schemata of assimilation and accommodation) by means of reflective abstraction from adult actions. This hypothesis would account for the great variability in social development and also for the apparent precocity of some children in the social domain.

## Metacognition

Another cognitive process area that has received much attention in recent years is metacognition and, in particular, the work on metamemory. We will look at only some of the highlights of the memory work here. As in other areas, a major stimulus in this domain was the work of Piaget and Inhelder (1973) on memory, which supported, with developmental data, Bartlett's (1932) demonstration that memory is an active reconstructive process and not simply a passive recording one. Much of the current research on memory and metamemory starts from the assumption that memory and memorizing are an active process. But recent studies on memory have had something of a different focus that should be highlighted.

In Piaget's and Bartlett's work, the memory processes explored were largely unconscious. In the Piaget and Inhelder studies, for example, memory improved as a consequence of changes in cognitive structure related to mental development. But work on memory and metamemory by Flavell and his colleagues (e.g., Flavell & Wellman, 1977) has had a different focus. These studies have been concerned with children's awareness of the memory process and their knowledge and use of strategies for reception, storage, and retrieval of material to be memorized.

As Flavell and Wellman (1977) point out, research on memory has to take into account (a) the strategies or mechanisms used by children as they go about trying to learn or remember, (b) task variables (the nature of the material to be retained or recalled), and (c) person variables (traits, background, etc.). Much of the recent work on memory is concerned with the first issue and looks at what these strategies are and how they change as a consequence of age and experience. But there is also considerable work being done on the task variables and on the person.

Very briefly, children's knowledge of and tendency to use memory strategies improves with age. Older children, for example, report some of the same retrieval strategies as younger children but also devise new and more sophisticated strategies and procedures than do the younger children. Such strategies include trying to reconstruct the events of an entire day in order to find the place where an object was lost. Clearly, the ability to reconstruct the day requires advanced cognitive abilities, while the use of such reconstruction for aid in recall is clearly a kind of "meta" cognition—using thinking to aid thinking.

As far as the task itself goes, much of the research in this area supports that from other domains. Namely, the more organizers available in the material to be learned, the more likely it is to be retained and recalled. Material is best retained when the learner can make categorical or conceptual linkages with the conceptual system and knowledge base that has previously been acquired. Although this finding is well established, devising means for assessing the knowledge base and matching material to it for the most efficient learning and recall remains a task for the future.

*Person variables in memory research* have been looked at developmentally rather than individually. The memory span of younger children is less than that of older children. Yet in some tasks, such as visual memory for pictures, younger children may have better memory than older children. Individual differences in memory capacity have not been explored very much, but it is clear that individuals differ enormously in memory capacity and usage. Perhaps the current interest in gifted children will promote more systematic investigation of individual memory processing. Why do some people retain almost everything they experience, while others retain almost nothing? Why do still others remember fully for specific tasks but forget everything once the task is accomplished? This, by the way, would be an interesting topic to explore with students.

Before I move on to another topic, it is perhaps appropriate to mention a personal reservation about metacognition. Memory is a very special case of cognitive processing in that it is self-conscious almost by definition. The individual intentionally and actively seeks to retrieve information. But memory is the exception in this regard and not the rule. Most of our cognitive processing is unconscious (Piaget's intellective unconscious) and is really not available to introspection. Children's explanations for their own and other's behavior are often farfetched. In general, I believe that we have to be very cautious about the validity of self-knowledge that has been obtained by reflection and introspection (Elkind, 1980).

## Role Taking

The next topic considered is the issue of role taking, which was once the fulcrum of social cognitive research. It was assumed that role taking was an ingredient basic to all social communicative skills. The work of Mead (1934), for example, suggested that the concept of self derived from the reflected appraisals of others. And Piaget (1932) argued that mutual respect and reciprocity came from interacting with peers and from learning to take their points of view. There were good reasons, therefore, for assuming that role taking and/or perspective taking were critical to the child's social development.

A great deal of research on role taking has now been done, and the issues and conceptualizations have been well defined. Some excellent reviews of the research in this area are also available (Chandler, 1976; Higgins, 1980; Shantz, 1975), so that ground need not be covered in great detail here. Rather, what I would like to do is emphasize some of the reservations about the role-taking literature that are currently emerging. My impressions are that much reconceptualization and reinterpretation of the data in this area are currently underway and that we should be aware of this ferment in presenting the material to students.

First of all, the basic data on perspective and role taking—namely, that it is not until children have attained concrete operations that they can take another person's perspective when it is different from their own—will probably hold up. Where the controversy arises is in research investigations purporting to show that even children as young as age two can do some perspective taking. Clearly, the perspective taking at this level is different from that at older age levels, but it is still considered perspective taking by some investigators.

One task in such research involves presenting children with cards with different pictures on the two sides. While the child is looking at one side, he or she is asked whether a person opposite sees the same thing. Even children three years old appreciate that the other person does not see the same thing. Other evidence for early perspective taking comes from findings that four-year-olds talk baby talk to younger children (Shatz & Gelman, 1973) and to dolls and are aware that one must switch registers of speech when talking to younger people and dolls.

But the real question concerns what processes are being employed by children in such situations. Is it really a beginning stage of the perspective taking required by a three-mountains task or a right–left task? It could be, for example, that children learn certain social "frames," or expectancies (Elkind, in press) that have nothing to do with perspective taking. Children might learn, largely by abstraction from adults' behavior in relation to themselves, that you switch registers with people smaller than yourself. Likewise, in the picture task the young children may be having trouble with the pronouns (I, you, he, she) used by the investigator. In this task, verbal confusion may be confounded with perspective-taking ability.

The more central, and critical, question, however, is the extent to which perspective taking (putting oneself in another person's physical position) and role taking (putting oneself in another person's psychological position) are the necessary prerequisites for social understanding and development. Unfortunately, this seems to be the unquestioned assumption underlying and, indeed, justifying much of the research on role taking and perspective taking. It suggests that the child is the prime actor in the achievement of the social self. But, as Baumrind (1980) points out, there is much evidence to suggest that socialization is adult-mediated by means other than role taking and perspective taking.

This comment relates back to an earlier statement about mediated learning experiences and the role of the adult as part of the child's adaptive apparatus. The real problem with the perspective/role-taking approach is its minimization of the role of adult mediation in social learning. Socialization is first and foremost the learning of the rules, understandings, and expectancies that operate in repetitive social situations. The "frames" are communicated by adults in a myriad of ways: raised eyebrows, voice tone, gesture, and so on. Role and perspective taking probably play a small part in learning frames, while reflective abstraction from adult behavior is a much more probable candidate. It seems likely that children attain social understanding more by having abstracted common social frames than because they have tried to put themselves in the positions of others.

## Language Development

Again, as in the case of cognition, an attempt to describe recent trends in language development research has to be selective. In general, one can say that the influence of Chomsky (1975) is somewhat diminished and that the concern with the development of grammars, once so prominent, has lessened. There is much more concern these days with semantics, with meaning, and with language in its functional sense. There seems to be more interest in language as communication than as an abstract rule system.

I will review several directions of research. One is children's use of orientational terms such as *front* and *back, on top of,* and so forth. Another is the use of language in specific situations and frames. A related area of interest is a concern with individual differences in language patterns and strategies. Stimulated by the need for bilingual education, there is renewed interest in second-language learning. Finally, the capacity of higher apes to learn language has been challenged, and a considerable debate is in progress as to what apes can and cannot do.

## Orientational Terms

The study of children's use of orientational terms is but one aspect of an approach that asks how children map language onto their cognitive constructions. At the heart of this approach is Piaget's (1967) notion that, at least in the early years, language development patterns itself after the child's own conceptual constructions. One example of this approach is found in the work of Nelson (1975a), who found that some of children's first language utterances—"more cookie" and "all gone"—appear soon after children have discovered conservation of objects. "All gone" deals with the disappearance of objects, while "more cookie" deals with their expected reappearance.

Recent work suggests that orientation words also map the child's cognitive, or nonlinguistic, strategies in relation to objects. Clark (1980), for example, found that children have a strong preference for the top or uppermost surface of objects. Because of this preference they responded more correctly to the term *top* than to *bottom, front,* or *back.* Clark claims that in order to be sure a child truly understands a term, as opposed to associating it by chance with a preferred strategy, one has to wait until the child can contrast terms like *top* and *bottom* and *front* and *back.* Without such contrasts, one cannot be sure that the child truly understands the orientational terms.

A general conclusion from this line of research is that the sequence in which children acquire orientational terms follows the sequence of their cognitive constructions. Apparently it is not correct to say that there are linguistic asymmetries in such pairs as *top* and *bottom* or *front* and *back* such that one dominates the other and is used as a synonym. Rather, it appears that while there may be conceptual asymmetries, these do not make for asymmetries in the acquisition of words. Children use nonlinguistic strategies as a basis for their linguistic understanding, and their language use reflects the development of these strategies.

## Language Situations

The question for investigators working in the domain of language situations involves the discrepancy between the sophistication of young children's language usage and their relative naivete with respect to many cognitive issues such as conservation. How is it that young children use inference, prediction, and long-term memory in their linguistic constructions and not in their cognitive constructions?

One way of approaching this problem is with script, or frame, theory borrowed from sociology and anthropology. Scripts, or frames, are models of repeated and familiar experiences that come into play in the appropriate verbal or situational context. Each script (a) contains certain basic obligatory events in sequence, (b) predicts open slots for optional objects and events and what they may contain, and (c) designates appropriate roles and actors.

Many scripts or frames can be identified. There are the "goodbye" frame, the "going to bed" frame, and the "thank you" frame. Even young children seem to learn those frames that constitute a structure for action, inference, and prediction. Put differently, by learning frames through repeated experience, the child can use that external structure for his or her verbal utterances. In effect, the utilization of frames enables the child to use language in ways that map the frame rather than the child's own cognitive structure.

Hence we now have, thanks to Nelson (1978), an intriguing explanation of a phenomenon that has baffled child watchers for a decade. The explanation, like all good explanations, is a simple one. The child uses environmental regularities to map language as well as internal cognitive constructions. But there is another explanation, namely, the one suggested earlier. If language is a "mediating structure" acquired from adults by reflective abstraction from their language behavior, we would have an account of child language precocity congruent, rather than in conflict, with cognitive developmental theory.

## Individual Differences

Children clearly differ in their language usage. But how are these differences to be described and explained? In one sense the concern with individual differences can be viewed as an offshoot of the concern with dialects and with bilingualism. But there are also speech patterns that are more individual than either dialect or second-language fluency, and these also require investigation.

Early studies of individual differences in language were primarily concerned with language precocity and delay. Early speech was generally associated with high intelligence and delayed speech with low intelligence. Sex differences in language ability and usage have also been explored, most recently at the infancy level. But the results vary so much from study to study (e.g., Anastasi & D'Angelo, 1952; Anastasi & DeJesus, 1953) that it is hard to formulate any clear-cut issue on this matter.

In a series of studies Nelson (1975b) suggests that at least some individual differences in speech patterns are derived from the way in which the mother talks to her child. Nelson says that *expressive* speakers use a good balance of nouns and pronouns and use more complex sentence structures than do children whom Nelson calls *referential* speakers. Children who are referential in their speech patterns tend to use more nouns than pronouns and are also more likely to label than to describe (as expressive children do).

Other investigators are beginning to describe individual differences in language use. Wolf and Gardner (1979), for example, distinguish between patterners and dramatists. This is a content distinction as opposed to Nelson's more functional description. That is, *patterners* are children who in their speech are primarily concerned with describing objects and relations in the real world. *Dramatists,* in contrast, tend to focus in their speech on interpersonal relations and to tell stories with a beginning, middle, and end. Obviously everyone at times is a patterner or a dramatist, but children do seem to show a marked preference for one or another mode of expression. Clearly, much more work needs to be done in this area of individual differences.

## Bilingual Learning

The civil rights movement was perhaps the single most important event that triggered active interest in second-language learning. One focus of criticism growing out of that movement was the fact that the schools were not providing for the linguistic diversity of the children they served. It began to be recognized that black children often spoke a different dialect than white children and that Spanish-speaking or Indian-language-speaking children were at a disadvantage in schools that did not recognize the bilingual problems these children were encountering.

As a consequence there has been a great increase in the interest in second-language learning. There has also been considerable federal legislation regarding the provision of bilingual education and not a little controversy regarding it. In addition, the issue of second-language learning also encompasses the problem of English-speaking students learning foreign languages in schools and colleges.

Unfortunately, many bilingual programs were instituted, particularly for Spanish-speaking children, without a good understanding of what a good second-languge learning program should be. As often happens in the case of federal mandates, programs are often instituted long before the research needed to make the programs effective has been done. In effect, these programs themselves become the research base, but they are of less value than if they had been designed to answer research questions.

The following brief descriptions of some of the findings of research on bilingual education during the past decade will serve to convey an impression of where we are now in this field: (a) The teaching of reading in a second language without prior oral training does not appear to be successful; (b) participation in bilingual programs does not retard the child's acquisition of his or her native language; (c) bilingual children have an initial disadvantage and a slower learning rate than nonbilingual children; and (d) to be effective, a second-language learning program has to involve oral training from the beginning.

By and large, studies of the effects of bilingual education funded under Title VII have suggested that the programs have not been successful in improving the academic achievement of bilingual children. Although these findings have been challenged, nearly everyone agrees that the bilingual programs have not met their designated goals.

The problems of bilingual education are extraordinarily complex inasmuch as they involve culture, motivation, childrearing, and much more. Motivation, for example, is critical to second-language learning, but it may not be strong in children who live in Spanish-speaking or dialect-speaking communities. In addition, polyglot languages such as "Tex Mex" or "Porcho" allow children to communicate in both English and Spanish but never expose them to correct standard English or Spanish. Such children are likely to be disadvantaged in both languages. There is a tremendous need for good solid research in second-language learning, and such research is only now beginning to be carried out. It could, by the way, teach us something about language learning in general.

## Ape Language

The history of psychologists trying to teach apes to talk is a long one. Early attempts were unsuccessful largely because the investigators sought to teach the apes to vocalize. But in the 1960s a new sort of study appeared in which apes were taught to communicate with signs, symbols, or mechanical means. Such studies did not identify language with speech and suggested that apes had the manual but not the vocal dexterity to communicate. Once taught a system, it was claimed, apes could do what true language speakers do—namely, create new words and word orders. They could even teach one another signs.

In the last few years, however, these findings have been challenged. Some investigators (Terrace, Petito, Sanders, & Bever, 1979) claim that the apes never learned language at all but, like the famous "Clever Hans," used cues unconsciously being given them by their trainers. Claims that apes had true generative communicative systems were attacked with reevaluation of tapes and data from early investigations. The controversy is still very active, and the verdict is not yet in. But it does look like some of the claims about ape communicative abilities will have to be modified and made more conservative.

# Conclusion

After rereading what I have written, I feel that I have left out so much that I have really not done justice to the subject. Indeed, I have not even kept tightly to my own guiding principles of selection. "Where the unconscious chooses, the conscious loses," I suppose. In any case, some of what is happening in developmental psychology today has been briefly presented. How to incorporate it into lectures and presentations is another matter.

I have only one suggestion for how the material might be used. I have focused on controversy, not so much because I was advocating one position over another but rather because it exemplifies the nature of scientific work. The work on role taking and the work on ape language are cases in point. Data are gathered, interpretations are made, and then new data and new interpretations are offered that contradict the old. There is change, but there is constancy too. The data, if they are solid, remain. Only the interpretations change.

It seems to me that college students need to have a chance to see how science works and that there is constancy and change to it. The tendency of the young is to criticize totally: If any part is wrong, so is the whole. What these examples might do is help students appreciate how science works and learn how to be critical but also constructive. In developmental psychology, as in all areas, it is important not to throw away solid data for want of a good theory.

## Reference Notes

1. Elkind, D., & Behmer, D. *The child's conception of the clergy.* Unpublished manuscript (Eliot-Pearson Department of Child Study Research Series, No. 2), Tufts University, 1981.
2. Edelstein, W., Keller, M., & Wahlen, K. *Structure and content in social cognition.* Paper presented at the Sixth Biennial Southeastern Conference on Human Development, Alexandria, Virginia, April 19, 1980.
3. Elkind, D. *Developmental psychology and education.* Paper presented at the dedication of the Lindquist Center, University of Iowa, Iowa City, September 6, 1980.

## References

Anastasi, A., & D'Angelo, R. Y. A comparison of Negro and white preschool children in language development. *Journal of Genetic Psychology,* 1952, *82,* 147–165.

Anastasi, A., & DeJesus, C. Language development and nonverbal IQ of Puerto Rican preschool children in New York City. *Journal of Abnormal and Social Psychology,* 1953, *48,* 357–366.

Bartlett, F. C. *Remembering.* London: Cambridge University Press, 1932.

Baumrind, P. New directions in socialization research. *American Psychologist,* 1980, *35,* 639–652.

Case, R. Intellectual development from birth to adulthood: A neo-Piagetian interpretation. In R. S. Siegler (Ed.), *Children's thinking: What develops.* Hillsdale, N.J.: Erlbaum, 1978.

Chandler, M. J. Social cognition: A selective review of current research. In W. Overton & J. Gallagher (Eds.), *Knowledge and development* (Vol. 1). New York: Plenum, 1976.

Chomsky, N. *Reflections on language.* New York: Pantheon, 1975.

Clark, E. V. Here's the top: Nonlinguistic strategies in the acquisition of orientational terms. *Child Development,* 1980, *51,* 329–338.

Elkind, D. On the validity of reflective knowledge. In R. V. Hannaford (Ed.), *Concept formation and explanation of behavior.* Ripon, Wisc.: Ripon College Press, 1980.

Elkind, D. Child development and early childhood education: Where we stand today. *Young Children,* in press.

Feuerstein, R. *Instrumental enrichment.* Baltimore: University Park Press, 1980.

Flavell, J. H., & Wellman, H. M. Metamemory. In R. V. Kail, Jr., & S. W. Hagen (Eds.), *Perspectives on the development of memory and cognition.* Hillsdale, N.J.: Erlbaum, 1977.

Furth, H. *The world of grownups: Children's conceptions of society.* New York: Elsevier, 1980.

Habermass, J. *Toward a rational society.* Boston: Beacon Press, 1970.

Habermass, J. *Zur Genese der Interaktionskompetenz.* Starnberg: Max Planck Institut zur Er forschung der lebens bedingungan der Wisserschaftlichtechnischen Welt, 1974. (mimeo)

Higgins, E. T. Role taking and social judgment: Alternative developmental perspectives and processes. In J. H. Flavell & L. Ross (Eds.), *New directions in the study of social cognitive development.* Cambridge, England: Cambridge University Press, 1980.

Kohlberg, L. Moral stages and moralization: The cognitive developmental approach. In T. Lickona (Ed.), *Moral development and behavior.* New York: Holt, Rinehart and Winston, 1976.

Kohlberg, L. Revisions in the theory and practice of moral development. In W. Damon (Ed.), *Moral development: New directions for child development* (Number I). San Francisco: Jossey Bass, 1978.

Mead, G. H. *Mind, self and society.* Chicago: University of Chicago Press, 1934.

Nelson, K. Concept, word, and sentence: Interrelations in acquisition and development. *Psychological Review,* 1975, *81,* 267–285. (a)

Nelson, K. Individual differences in early semantic and syntactic development. *Annals of the New York Academy of Sciences,* 1975, *263,* 132–139. (b)

Nelson, K. How children represent knowledge of their world in and out of language: A preliminary report. In R. S. Siegler (Ed.), *Children's thinking: What develops.* Hillsdale, N.J.: Erlbaum, 1978.

Pascual-Leone, J. A mathematical model for the transition rule in Piaget's developmental stages. *Acta Psychologica,* 1970, *63,* 301–345.

Perrin, E. There's a demon in your belly: Children's understanding of the causes, treatment and prevention of illness. Unpublished master's thesis, University of Rochester, 1981.

Piaget, J. *The moral judgment of the child.* New York: Harcourt Brace, 1932.

Piaget, J. *Six psychological studies.* New York: Random House, 1967.

Piaget, J., & Inhelder, B. *Memory and intelligence.* New York: Basic Books, 1973.

Selman, R. Toward a structural analysis of developing interpersonal relations. In A. D. Pick (Ed.), *Minnesota Symposium on Child Psychology.* Minneapolis: University of Minnesota Press, 1976.

Selman, R. L. *The growth of interpersonal understanding.* New York: Academic Press, 1980.

Selman, R. L., & Jacquette, D. Stability and oscillation in interpersonal awareness. A clinical-developmental analysis. In C. B. Keasey (Ed.), *Nebraska Symposium on Motivation* (Vol. 25). Lincoln: University of Nebraska Press, 1979.

Shantz, C. U. The development of social cognition. In E. M. Hetherington (Ed.), *Review of child development research,* (Vol. 5). Chicago: University of Chicago Press, 1975.

Shatz, M., & Gelman, R. The development of communication skills: Modifications in the speech of young children as a function of listener. *Monographs of the Society for Research in Child Development,* 1973, *38,* No. 5, Serial No. 152.

Siegler, R. S. The origins of scientific reasoning. In R. S. Siegler (Ed.), *Children's thinking: What develops.* Hillsdale, N.J.: Erlbaum, 1978.

Terrace, H. S., Petito, L. A., Sanders, R.J., & Bever, T. G. Can an ape create a sentence? *Science,* 1979, *206,* 891–902.

Weisz, J. R. Autonomy, control and other reasons why "Mom is the Greatest." A content analysis of children's Mothers' Day letters. *Child Development,* 1980, *51,* 801–807.

Wolf, D., & Gardner, H. Style and sequence in early symbolic play. In R. N. Smith & M. B. Franklin (Eds.), *Early symbolization.* Hillsdale, N.J.: Erlbaum, 1979.

WALTER MISCHEL

# CURRENT ISSUES AND CHALLENGES IN PERSONALITY

W alter Mischel is presently professor of psychology at Stanford University, a position he has held since 1962. He earned his doctorate in clinical psychology in 1956 at Ohio State University and subsequently held faculty positions at the University of Colorado and Harvard University before moving to Stanford. His research has distinguished him as one of the leading authorities in the area of personality. Among his numerous publications are three books on personality, including *Introduction to Personality,* originally published in 1971 and now in its third edition. Delay of gratification, the nature of rewards, sex differences, and personality assessment are some of the topics that Mischel has researched. More recently his efforts have focused on the interface of cognition and personality.

A fellow of the American Psychological Association since 1968, Mischel has been active in the affairs of that Association as well as other professional societies. In 1978, he was given the Distinguished Scientist Award by APA's Division of Clinical Psychology (Section III). Earlier honors include distinguished lectureships at Kansas State University, the University of Michigan, Ohio University, and the University of Hawaii.

While Mischel is principally identified with the field of personality research, his expertise in other areas such as social psychology, developmental psychology, cognition, and clinical psychology is evidenced by the many consultantships he has held with publishers and journals in those areas. In 1977, he demonstrated the diversity of his psychological interests with the publication of an introductory psychology text, *Essentials of Psychology* (with H. N. Mischel), a text now in its second edition. This diverse background in psychology is illustrated in this paper as Mischel treats recent trends in personality.

# CURRENT ISSUES AND CHALLENGES IN PERSONALITY

L et me begin by sharing a few orienting comments about the under-graduate teaching of personality. Later I will try to give a sense of how I see some of the main developments in the field that now merit attention at the undergraduate level.

## Psychology as a Unified Field

For a period of about 25 years I have tried to remain involved with undergraduate education, as reflected in my textbooks as well as in my own teaching (Mischel, 1981; Mischel & Mischel, 1980). I think my reason for doing this is not simply sadomasochism. For me, under-graduate teaching, and particularly undergraduate teaching at the survey levels, provides a great challenge and an opportunity to do something seriously about attempting to keep psychology (or to make psychology) a unified field. I grew up in a psychology that, at the time of my education in the 1950s, was still serious about the possibility of an integrated and unified discipline. I hope it is not merely nostalgia that still makes me believe it is worth trying to keep the teaching of psychology, and the structure of psychology, as integrated and as unified as possible. The pursuit of such integration and unification not only has didactic advantages but is important for us in our roles as psychologists and scientists.

I become concerned whenever APA adds another division, and the divisions keep multiplying. And I am distressed when I cannot see the connection between the seemingly fractured parts of most introductory psychology texts. These fragmented texts seem to mirror the divisions (literally) of the profession of psychologists rather than offering a sense of the underlying unity and integrity of our science.

Before addressing new developments in personality, let me say just a few words about what I see as the essence of that unity and integrity. I have remained committed to the belief that there are a number of basic principles (many of which we probably have not yet found but which await our invention or construction) that apply to the total discipline, regardless of the different content areas of the field. So whatever the principles are that lead a child, let us say, to develop a strong tendency to drown cats, those same principles should also help us to understand why another child becomes altruistic. Whatever the principles are that underlie how we get to be the people we are ought also to be the principles we need to harness when we try to understand the process of treatment-induced change. The hope here is that the principles that underlie development and growth are the same principles that underlie change and that we need in order to understand the interactions between people in real life and in the situations that social psychologists study. This search for underlying principles is my emphasis in teaching and underlies how I organize my own presentation of introductory psychology in textbook form (Mischel & Mischel, 1980).

## Necessary Background: Four Traditions

My main mission in this lecture is to offer some glimpses into the field of personality worth conveying to undergraduate students. In the field of personality, there are four traditions, or main areas, that I feel are important to present to students as background. One area deals with measurement and intelligence. It seems to me that the contributions that have come from psychometrics, and particularly from the application of psychometrics to the measurement of intelligence, are enduring. These applications have been around for 70–80 years, and they are well worth teaching to our students. These same notions about intelligence testing were extended by trait psychologists who wanted to use the same orientation and the same way of measuring to study character, personality traits, and social dispositions. That extension represents, I think, a second important tradition that needs to be brought seriously to the attention of our students. So the first area is psychometrics and intelligence, and the second is the application of psychometrics to the measurement of traits and types (i.e., to the measurement of social and personological dispositions).

The third area that requires attention, even at the level of a survey course, is the search for motives, particularly the psychodynamically oriented search for motives. This search refers to the effort to find a way to infer motivational dispositions that would get beneath the surface of behavior, that would penetrate the patina to uncover one's unconscious processes, distortions, and aspects. Psychologists in this tradition attempted to infer underlying motivational dispositions indirectly, through various kinds of subtle techniques (e.g., projective tests and depth interviews), in order to illuminate the motivational structure of individuals. The psychodynamic approach and the challenges and issues that it raises are of sufficient importance not only within psychology but in other disciplines and in everyday life to merit the attention of undergraduates.

The fourth area that requires coverage comprises two different positions that are often thought of as being in some kind of competition or war with each other. Actually these two views have some curious affinities as well as some intense animosities. I am referring here to the enduring dialogue between the behavioristic movement on the one hand and the cognitive-phenomenological-self orientation on the other. At the teaching level, this is the dialogue or "debate," if you will, between behaviorism and humanism. An attempt to achieve a reconciliation between these two approaches is an important teaching objective for me.

In sum, then, there are four major areas or traditions in the field of personality that I think require coverage at the beginning undergraduate level: the measurement of intelligence; the application of basic measurement strategies in the search for traits and types; the search for underlying motives from a psychodynamic perspective; and, finally, the dialogue between behaviorism and humanism, or between behavioral and more cognitive- and phenomenological-self oriented approaches.

In teaching, I try to illustrate the strengths and weaknesses of these four approaches by applying each of them to the analysis of the same case material. In this way, students can see exactly how each of these approaches would attempt to measure the same person, and they are exposed to concrete case summaries about the same individual analyzed from each of these major perspectives.

## New Developments in Personality

With these broad orientations as background, what is new in the field in the last five years? From my vantage point, the answer is a great deal.

### Traits

First, much attention continues to be given to the nature of traits, what they are, how you infer them, and what their uses are for both psychologists and laypersons. As you all know, trait psychology has historically been committed to the proposition that individual differences exist in the form of generalized, enduring dispositions. A personality trait has to have two characteristics: It has to be enduring over time, and it has to have a considerable amount of generality across situations. That means that somebody who is "friendly" ought to be friendly not only over lengthy periods of time when measured in the same context by the same instrument but also ought to display friendliness across a number of situations in which friendliness is to be expected. How broad or specific are traits really? Psychologists have been debating this question literally since the days of G. Stanley Hall. It is perhaps the oldest issue in the field—Thorndike was worrying about it in 1904, Hartshorne and May got into it in the 1920s, and the issue just does not go away—and I do not think it *will* go away.

My own approach to this debate when I teach undergraduates is to give a bit of an account of my own research history and to tell students about the trials and tribulations that I went through in my own work and how I bit my own fingernails when trying to answer this question from my data. The stories that I tell my students on this topic deal with my effort to study delay of gratification as a personality disposition. That story began for me in the late 1950s when I did some cross-cultural fieldwork in the West Indies. This work on delaying of gratification really began as a kind of afterthought, because I originally was interested in the problem of the relationships among what people think, what they do, and what they feel or experience. I was interested in these three levels: deep experience, self-report, and behavior—that is, what you really feel, what you say you feel, and what you do. Indeed, I think that those three levels have continued to be an abiding interest for me, but I wanted to study them (if I may indulge in a bit of autobiography for a moment) in another culture, a culture in which the fascinating practice of spirit possession was to be found. To study the three levels, I went to the Caribbean to the island of Trinidad, where spirit possession in the form of the Shango Cult, as it was then called, was practiced in the 1950s. My (naive) idea was that I would see what the people in the cult did normally when they were not in a trance and that would tell me about action. (Please, remember this was 25 years ago, so be merciful when judging the research design.) Then I would give them projective tests to find out what they were "really" experiencing, thinking, and feeling at a "deeper level." So I brought my Rorschach blots and TAT cards and so on to find out about the deep structure. Then I would also ask them for their own self-reports on various measures. I hoped that we could assess behavior when the person was not possessed, that we could assess behavior when the person was possessed (by watching the individuals during ceremonies), that we could get a "deep" view of underlying motives, needs, and so on, through projective devices, and that we could also get at the self-report level by asking directly. It seemed a fantastic set-up! It took me about three weeks to find out how naive I was.

What we were getting on the projective tests (particularly the Thematic Apperception Test), for example, turned out to be mostly stories about cowboy movies. Our local informants knew, of course, that we were from the United States, and they thought they should tell us what we would be interested in hearing. So we got all kinds of nice stories about things they thought we would like to hear (e.g., current U.S. films) rather than deep revelations of underlying processes. (Or, if we were getting deep revelations of underlying processes, we did not know how to unscramble them.) So I stopped doing that and looked instead at how these people were characterizing themselves and each other.

A dimension that people in the village seemed to be using a great deal in describing their everyday life involved delay of gratification. They described some of their neighbors as impulsive, never knowing how to wait for anything; they characterized others as always hiding their money under the bed, planning for the future, and delaying immediate gratification for long-term goals. To tap this dimension, we developed simple choices for studying preferences for immediate smaller rewards or delayed larger rewards, and we proceeded to look for the correlates of that choice. For example, we gave children choices between a small candy bar now and a larger one later. We found that their preferences for immediate smaller rewards or delayed larger rewards did indeed have extensive networks of meaningful correlations. Some of the time these correlations were quite high (even as high as .50), but most of the time they tended to be modest (e.g., .30). These patterns allowed us to make some rather interesting generalizations about groups of people, but the results were not powerful enough to allow statements about *individuals*. I use that example with my students because it is prototypic of what so many of my colleagues were finding at around the same time—namely, that one can do a very nice job academically of devising an instrument for practically anything and treat it as a dimension on which individuals differ. One can then study the dimension by obtaining choices and self-reports (in the way that I am describing), or by making other kinds of scales, and look for the correlates. One could be very imaginative about it: One could look for childrearing correlates, or for sociocultural correlates, or for all kinds of other personal and social indices in the search for meaningful patterns.

I used the term *personality coefficient* to describe the coefficients, usually at about the .30 level (on the average, roughly speaking), that tend to emerge from research in this vein (Mischel, 1968). In recent years much effort has been devoted to showing that one can do better than that, and some of the results have been quite interesting. For example, Epstein (Note 1) has tried to improve data about traits by very carefully taking the reliability of measurement into account. Others try to make the measures as pure as possible (Block & Block, 1980). I think it is important to let our students know that such efforts are under way to improve the quality of research in the continuing quest for broad personality traits.

To summarize the results of these efforts briefly, it is becoming very clear that we can identify good temporal stabilities associated with personality to describe what people are like over time. Particularly if we use rating measures we are able to identify that the same person who, for example, is friendly today on a number of rating measures is likely also to be rated as relatively friendly even long periods of time later. The same is true for a large number of dispositions. So there is an increasing body of evidence suggesting that particularly when multiple measures are used, and when good scales are constructed, one can demonstrate impressive temporal stability in many personal and social dispositions.

The fact that good temporal stabilities are being documented has some important implications, I think, for how we teach aspects of personality development. It means that we have been getting good documentation in the last half dozen years for impressive continuities in personality over time. There is evidence that even at ages as young as 3 or 4 years, threads of continuity over time begin to be spun. This is a very encouraging piece of evidence to keep in mind when instructing undergraduates. There are discontinuities, of course (e.g., Baltes, 1980; Kagan, 1980), but there also are continuities. A good example here is the work of the Blocks (Block & Block, 1980) reported in the *Minnesota Symposium on Child Psychology*. They found continuities over fairly long periods of time (in their longitudinal study conducted at Berkeley) in two related traits: ego strength and ego resilience. This research is sound and is important enough to be brought to the attention of undergraduate students.

Let me summarize on the topic of consistency. I am saying that evidence for good continuity of temporal stability is becoming commonplace. But what about evidence for broad cross-situational consistency across contexts? When it comes to cross-situational breadth, that is, to the question of how generalized these dispositions may be, things get more thorny. Is the person who is likely to be friendly in one context also likely to be friendly in another, different context? I think here the answer becomes very complex and controversial, and the basic issues are still unresolved.

Recently there have been some vigorous defenses of traits. In the area of attitude consistency, Fishbein and Ajzen (1977; Ajzen & Fishbein, 1975) proposed that if we aggregate or pool measures and look for a close fit between the predictor and the criterion, we are going to do much better than if we do not take that fit into account.

Suppose, for instance, that you try to infer somebody's trait of friendliness. You might use a dozen different measures, each of which has a dozen subscales with many items on them, and you might average all of that together to get an aggregated (pooled) estimate of the disposition. If you want to use that estimate of the disposition to predict what the person will do and then try to predict for a specific act (such as whether the person will be friendly in a particular situation in one specific instance), you're not likely to do very well. But if you use an aggregated or pooled criterion (in which you assess friendliness over many trials or sample it with a large number of measures and pool them so that you now have an aggregated measure at the criterion end also), you are likely to make better predictions from the disposition. That is, with an aggregated measure at the criterion end and an aggregated measure at the predictor end, you are likely to do better. On the other hand, if you want to get very specific, if you want to predict what somebody's going to do in a particular situation now with regard to friendliness, probably the best estimate will be made from the closest, single specific approximation of behavior in that situation. For example, the person's specific previous behavior in the most closely related situations, or the person's own self-prediction of what he or she is likely to do in that situation, or the person's own intention statement about that situation may be the best predictors of the specific act.

The gist of this work is that there must be a fit between the predictor and the criterion. The message is that we should be as careful about how well we sample the criterion that we are trying to predict as we are about how well we sample the disposition that we are trying to infer. When there is a good match in the degree of generality/specificity between the predictor and the criterion, one is likely to predict better than when these two are poorly matched. So pooled criteria are likely to be predicted better by dispositional measures; single-act criteria are predicted best by a specific relevant predictor, and a good fit between predictor and criterion is important.

A related line of work proposes that trait consistency might be found but only in some of the people some of the time (e.g., Bem & Allen, 1974). Thus if one looks for subscales of people with regard to some dispositions, it might be possible to make useful statements that could not be made about all people on all traits. Bem and Allen's work on this is prototypic, and again, although it can be challenged, it is certainly a development worth discussing with undergraduates.

When teaching the trait approach, I try to emphasize that traits have both uses and misuses; we really cannot avoid making trait inferences about people, but when we do so we ought to be aware of what we gain and what we lose. Particularly when it comes to gross screening decisions (or trying to make statements about different groups of people), there is really no way of getting around making inferences about the group in general—that is, of trying to get some estimate of its central tendency. And it is certainly useful for some purposes to make central tendency estimates about groups of people. That kind of screening has been a basic need, goal, and activity in our field for 80 years. But on the other hand, for many purposes we do not want to talk about the group in general or about the aggregated or the average behavior of the person in general. We want to work with a much more microscopic, much more molecular vantage point, focusing on a specific interaction between what the individual is doing and what is happening to him or her. If, for example, we want to see a child in the context of his or her family, or a couple in relationship to each other, the personological focus on change and on the interaction between person and condition can be much more important than a focus on the central tendency. So there are two different purposes here that should not be mixed up. Some of the time we want to make generalizations about the individual or about the group "on the whole." There is no way to do that except to make central tendency estimates, which we get by doing good, reliable, clean research on central tendencies, on general dispositions, or on characteristics.

Some of the time, however, the emphasis is on trying to understand what the person is doing in context. When we do that, we do not want to aggregate or estimate central tendencies; we want to look at the fine-grained interactions happening in the context, and we want to be able to demonstrate how behavior changes as the context changes. The focus then becomes a focus on "functional analysis." It seems to me that one of the main contributions of the behavioral approach in the last 10 or 15 years has been to show us, in many instances rather beautifully, how such functional analysis operates. The work of Patterson (e.g., 1976) illustrates how what the child is doing with regard to aggression, for example, hinges exquisitely on what is happening to the child. One can make very reliable predictions, for instance, about how certain behaviors like teasing or whining from a sibling will reliably induce hitting behavior in the child. Clinical examples can demonstrate in interesting ways how even quite complicated patterns of behavior (like autism) hinge on what is happening to the person.

In summary, I think it is important to convey at least two points about the uses and misuses of traits. One is that if your interest is in making a central tendency or average statement about the person on the whole, or about the group on the whole, you should try to get the most reliable overall characterization possible with regard to the pattern of behavior in which you are interested. If, on the other hand, the focus is on understanding the relationship between what the person is doing and the context, then it becomes important to focus on functional relationships. Obviously, an understanding of what the person is doing in context is particularly important when one wants to attempt behavior therapy and behavior change.

One of the new developments in the study of traits and types concerns the notion of prototypicality, or "typical people." In work inspired by Rosch in cognitive psychology, Cantor and I (e.g., Cantor & Mischel, 1979) and Wiggins and others have been trying to look at traits in a somewhat different way. Rather than trying to identify all of the characteristics that belong in a dispositional category (e.g., all of the signs of "friendliness"), we have been trying to find the crucial ingredients, the central features, the prototypical qualities of the "typical" member of that category.

Consider first the domain of everyday common objects rather than people. As pointed out by Rosch (1977), when we try to think of, for example, a *bird*, the chances are high that what comes to mind is not a penguin or a chicken. The chances are high that what you will think about when you think about a bird is a robin or a sparrow; some kind of prototypical bird, an exemplar, comes to mind. Likewise, when we think about a chair, we are more likely to think about a kitchen chair than about an odd, peculiarly shaped three-legged chair. The same notion of prototype also seems to be useful in studying types like extraverts and introverts. That is, there might be person categories that also have a kind of naturalness to them, and one can identify the prototypical or basic features of such person categories, searching for the rules that people use in making decisions about whether somebody is an extravert or an introvert, for example. The questions here require studying what features are used and how they are put together in the perceiver's effort to identify who is a prototypical used-car seller, or comic joker, or jock, or extravert. Of course, we do not have to necessarily use the person categories of traditional trait theory. There may be person categories in everyday language that reflect more accurately what people do naturally. The possibility that we ought to be looking for good exemplars of typical people with regard to particular kinds of categories is to me an interesting idea worth serious attention.

## Social Ecology

In the last five years some researchers tried to move beyond the identification of person characteristics altogether to try to capture the crucial ingredients of environments. That is, they wanted to assess the settings rather than the people. There has been quite a bit of interesting work in this vein, which is sometimes called "social ecology." In a related direction, social psychologists have been trying to study "scripts" (e.g., Shank & Abelson, 1977). For many social situations, such as going to a restaurant, we seem to have scripts available. We know, for instance, that if we go into a MacDonald's we pay first and eat later, but if we go into a fine French restaurant, we order first and pay later. There are sequences of appropriate behavior in these scripts for simple social situations like going to a restaurant, having a birthday party, or visiting a physician. Children know about many of these scripts very early in life. And much of our behavior may be "scripted" and may run off in a fairly automatic and almost mindless way. Indeed, much of what we do may be guided by more or less automatic scripts that generate automatic behavior. This does not require invoking some kind of an "unconscious"; rather, it can be viewed as simply a habitual sequence that runs itself off, often rather mindlessly, and that does not require consciousness unless it becomes interrupted.

## Cognitive-Social Learning

From my point of view, to integrate personality psychology with developments in the rest of the field requires that we try to come up with a set of variables—ways of slicing individual differences—that will relate meaningfully to what we know about basic psychological processes. So it may be better not to talk about individual differences primarily on semantic dimensions (like "friendliness") but instead to describe such individual differences in ways that relate to basic psychological processes. For these purposes we need constructs about people that assess their competencies, encoding strategies, expectancies, subjective values, and plans (e.g., Mischel, 1973). We need to consider such variables in order to understand how individuals process information, make choices, and act interpersonally. By construing individual differences in ways that relate clearly to basic processes of learning and cognition, the more arbitrary divisions among our field may be reduced. In this "cognitive-social learning" framework, if we want to assess personality adequately we have to assess such variables as what the person expects is going to happen and his or her relevant competencies, constructs, and values. We also have to examine how plans and thoughts are translated into specific action depending on what people say to themselves and imagine.

To illustrate this approach, consider Sarason's (Note 2) recent studies of interfering self-preoccupying thoughts. His work suggests that anxiety interferes with successful test-taking when individuals start to say things to themselves like "I'm no good at this. I'll never be able to do it." In contrast, performance improves when one says, for example, "Now, I have to recheck my answers" while taking a test. This is an important point that has come from many different lines of research in the last half dozen years—from studies on learned helplessness, self-efficacy, and the impact of negative expectations about oneself. When people are engaged in negative thought processes, when they are making negative attributions, when they are saying "I can't do it" or "I don't know how" or "I'll never get it done" or "I'm no good at this," they are short-circuiting their own chances for effective performance. Test anxiety and many other kinds of performance problems seem to be the result of such negative cognitions.

The therapeutic implications have encouraged efforts at cognitive behavior modification. For example, Meichenbaum (1977) and colleagues note that impulsive children fail when they neglect to say to themselves, "I must stop now and check my work." Instead these children probably say all kinds of irrelevant, disruptive things to themselves that undermine their performance. Likewise, depressed people also often tend to distract themselves with all kinds of irrelevant thoughts and to make negative self-statements. They say, "I'll never do it, I'll never get it done, I'm no good. There is no point trying it. It's no use." The message here is that adequate performance is mediated by appropriate cognition. Successful performance requires positive expectations: Given adequate competency training, when people expect to do well, they do well, and when they expect to fail, they are more likely to fail. To catastrophize about one's own performance, to attribute failure to incorrigible shortcomings in oneself, to say, "I'm no good at this, I'll never be able to do it," is to assure further failure and ultimately a sense of apathy and depression (e.g., Seligman, 1975).

In related work, Dweck and her associates (Dweck, 1975; Diener & Dweck, 1978) have studied individual differences in children who show either a "helplessness" or a "mastery" orientation. Children who have a helplessness orientation are defined as those who characterize themselves in terms like "I don't know how to do it, I can't do it, I'm no good at it"; in other words, these are the children who expect to fail and attribute their failure to their own faults and personal shortcomings. In contrast, children with a mastery orientation are those who have strong self-efficacy expectations and attribute success to their own abilities and efforts. Children who are mastery-oriented as opposed to helplessness-oriented also display quite different ideation when they are engaged in the problem-solving process. The mastery-oriented children are the ones who tend to say, "The harder it gets, the harder I need to try," or they say, "I've almost got it now," or "I love a challenge," and they go on to solve the problem. The helplessness-oriented children are the ones who instead say, "I never did have a good memory, I'm getting confused now," and who then proceed to fail.

A good deal of research in the last four or five years has shown that on the whole it is good for us to believe that we can do something to control events. Much research suggests that when individuals believe they cannot control events and outcomes, they tend to develop a sense of helplessness and apathy. Conversely, when they are led to think that they can influence and control events, that they can make an impact on their environment, they then tend to become happier and more alert. Some work suggests that they might even live longer. The importance of this finding is that it is in agreement with findings from other studies of health, stress, illness, and well-being that suggest a link between cognition and total psychophysiological health.

A classic study in this area was done by Rodin and Langer in

1977. They gave a group of institutionalized elderly adults opportunities to make decisions actively and to be personally responsible for something outside of themselves (a simple green plant). These people soon began to act more competently, and to feel better, compared to groups of elderly institutionalized people stuck in the usual passive institutional routine in which all decisions were made for them by the staff. And a follow-up 18 months later suggested that only half as many had died in the active-responsibility group as in the comparison group. This study, while it has methodological problems, makes a very dramatic case for the importance of the perception of control as a mediator of health.

## Cognitive Economics

A final idea that I want to mention because of its importance in the undergraduate teaching of personality involves what I call cognitive economics. The growing recognition that there are severe limitations on the amount of information we can handle cognitively has some important social implications. Namely, there are all kinds of shortcuts that people automatically tend to take to reduce and simplify information. Sometimes these shortcuts oversimplify the information. Such oversimplification has costs as well as gains (Mischel, 1979). The gain is that we do not become overwhelmed by too much information. The loss is that we may be tempted into judgmental errors that perpetuate certain kinds of social stereotypes and that undermine how well we function as clinical judges. The gains and losses of cognitive economics for social behavior and interpersonal perception are sure to be a focus for much research in the next five years and probably will alter our conceptions of personality in ways that cannot yet be fully anticipated.

### Reference Notes

1. Epstein, S. *Behavioral consistency: Myth or reality?* Debate with W. Mischel presented at the meeting of the American Psychological Association, Montreal, Quebec, Canada, September 3, 1980.
2. Sarason, I. G. *Life stress, self-preoccupation, and social supports.* Presidential address delivered at the meeting of the Western Psychological Association, San Diego, California, April 1979.

### References

Ajzen, I., & Fishbein, M. Attitude-behavior relations: A theoretical analysis and review of empirical research. *Psychological Bulletin,* 1977, *84,* 888–918.

Baltes, P. B. Life-span developmental psychology: Observations on history and theory. In P. B. Baltes and O. G. Brim, Jr. (Eds.), *Life-span development and behavior*, (Vol. 2). New York: Academic Press, 1980.

Bem, D. J., & Allen, A. On predicting some of the people some of the time: The search for cross-situational consistencies in behavior. *Psychological Review*, 1974, *81*, 506–520.

Block, J., & Block, J. The role of ego control and ego resiliency in the organization of behavior. In W. A. Collins (Ed.), *The Minnesota Symposium on Child Psychology* (Vol. 13). Hillsdale, N.J.: Erlbaum, 1980.

Cantor, N., & Mischel, W. Prototypes in person perception. In L. Berkowitz (Ed.), *Advances in experimental social psychology*. New York: Academic Press, 1979.

Diener, C. I., & Dweck, C. S. An analysis of learned helplessness: Continuous changes in performance, strategy, and achievement cognitions following failure. *Journal of Personality and Social Psychology*, 1978, *36*, 451–462.

Dweck, C. S. The role of expectations and attributions in the alleviation of learned helplessness. *Journal of Personality and Social Psychology*, 1975, *31*, 674–685.

Fishbein, M., & Ajzen, I. *Belief, attitude, intention and behavior*. Reading, Mass.: Addison-Wesley, 1975.

Kagan, J. Perspectives on continuity. In O. G. Brim, Jr., & J. Kagan (Eds.), *Constancy and change in human development*. Cambridge, Mass.: Harvard University Press, 1980.

Meichenbaum, D. (Ed.). *Cognitive-behavior modification: An integrative approach*. New York: Plenum Press, 1977.

Mischel, W. *Personality and assessment*. New York: Wiley, 1968.

Mischel, W. Toward a cognitive social learning reconceptualization of personality. *Psychological Review*, 1973, *80*, 252–283.

Mischel, W. On the interface of cognition and personality: Beyond the person-situation debate. *American Psychologist*, 1979, *34*, 740–754.

Mischel, W. *Introduction to personality* (3rd ed.). New York: Holt, Rinehart and Winston, 1981.

Mischel, W., & Mischel, H. N. *Essentials of psychology* (2nd ed.). New York: Random House, 1980.

Patterson, G. R. Aggressive child: Victim and architect of a coercive system. In E. J. Marsh, L. A. Hammerlynch, & L. C. Handy (Eds.), *Behavior modification and families*. New York: Bruner-Mazel, 1976.

Rodin, J., & Langer, E. Long-term effect of control-relevant intervention. *Journal of Personality and Social Psychology*, 1977, *35*, 897–902.

Rosch, E. Principles of categorization. In E. Rosch & B. B. Lloyd (Eds.), *Cognition and categorization*. Potomac, Md: Erlbaum, 1977.

Seligman, M. E. P. *Helplessness—On depression, development, and death*. San Francisco: W. H. Freeman, 1975.

Shank, R., & Abelson, R. *Scripts, plans, goals, and understanding*. Hillsdale, N.J.: Erlbaum, 1977.

# CLINICAL INTERVENTION: NEW DEVELOPMENTS IN METHODS AND EVALUATION

J erome L. Singer is professor of psychology and director of the Clinical Psychology Training Program at Yale University. In addition, he serves as co-director of the Yale University Family Television Research and Consultation Center. After completing his doctorate in clinical psychology in 1950 at the University of Pennsylvania, he worked for five years as a psychologist with the Veterans Administration Hospital in Montrose, New York. He left Montrose to pursue psychoanalytic training at the prestigious William Alanson White Institute of Psychiatry, Psychoanalysis, and Psychology. Since 1959 he has held academic positions at Teachers College of Columbia University, Adelphi University, and the City University of New York before assuming his present position at Yale in 1972.

Singer's interests are wide-ranging; he has published on the topics of projective testing, schizophrenia, female sexuality, television violence, psychotherapy, personality, REM sleep deprivation, and children's play. However, he is probably best known for his extensive research and writing in the area of daydreaming. His bibliography includes more than 100 papers in scientific journals and 10 books, plus another four books in progress. Many of these deal with daydreaming, fantasy, and imagery as they relate to personality, cognition, development, and creativity. His work has pioneered new methods in psychotherapy, a fact best illustrated by two of his books: *Imagery and Daydream Methods in Psychotherapy* (1974) and *The Power of Human Imagination: New Methods of Psychotherapy* (with K. Pope, 1978). Singer's expertise in imagery, psychotherapy, and psychoanalysis are ideally suited to the task of summarizing and evaluating recent developments in clinical intervention, which he does in this paper.

# CLINICAL INTERVENTION: NEW DEVELOPMENTS IN METHODS AND EVALUATION

T he decade that began in 1970 was not one that reflected great progress for American or international ideals, industrial development, or social reform. Against this background of hesitation and indecision at the global level, the opportunity to present news of modest but significant advances in scientific research and application in clinical psychology provides a welcome contrast. Psychologists have taken useful steps in applying the best available scientific knowledge to improve their psychotherapeutic procedures with a wide range of clients, increasingly emphasizing a problem-focused rather than a diffuse treatment orientation. New developments in the study of psychophysiological patterns, biofeedback, and self-regulatory mechanisms have led to the emergence of a new field of application, health psychology, within the broader domain of behavioral medicine. This new enterprise has important implications not only for *amelioration* of maladjustment but for *prevention* of physical as well as psychological distress. Finally, psychologists have continued to show leadership in the mental health area by developing increasingly ingenious and useful methods for evaluating intervention procedures and studying the processes of psychotherapy. As treatment costs in medicine and social welfare continue to soar, we can anticipate greater national concerns about accountability and cost-benefit analyses. Psychologists have taken important steps to develop a technology for evaluating psychotherapy and will undoubtedly play a key role in meeting the challenge of demonstrating the utility of specific treatment procedures.

This paper does not attempt a broad survey of *all* forms of clinical intervention. The field of community psychology, born in the turmoil of the 1960s, has suffered some setbacks but continues to thrive. Clinical and social psychologists who operate in this sphere are developing more precise terminology and specifying operations more carefully so as to permit measurement of their activities and assessment of their intervention effects. Moos's (1974) techniques for scoring the social atmosphere of various environments (e.g., a classroom, a hospital ward) have made possible the establishment of baseline data for identifying process and outcome of change efforts following systematic consultation or restructuring of power relations. Programs that involve training police officers in humane and psychologically sensitive approaches to resolving family disputes have begun to have an impact (Bard, 1971). A variety of such community or agency-oriented interventions have been documented in Rapaport's (1977) significant textbook.

This presentation focuses, however, on intervention with the individual client. If one takes a lofty vantage point, individual psychotherapy seems somehow a socially inefficient and, indeed, elitist approach to the amelioration of widespread personal maladjustment or emotional distress. We can never produce enough qualified therapists to provide one-on-one therapy for every person who has some sort of hang-up or personality quirk, nor even enough for the more seriously disturbed—the schizophrenics, addicts, and alcoholics. Yet our society, built around the core value of the individual, demands that such treatment be available. Given the opportunity, persons from lower socioeconomic backgrounds prefer individual therapy and profit from it (Goldstein, 1973; Lerner, 1972). Indeed, the exigencies of providing individualized treatment for an ever-widening clientele have forced psychologists to develop more efficient, problem-focused treatment orientations that are, I believe, improving our understanding of the therapeutic process and of the match between symptom, client, and therapeutic orientation (Goldstein & Stein, 1976).

# Developments in Individual Psychotherapy Practice

*Psychoanalysis and the Psychodynamic Therapies*

In one form or another the psychodynamic orientation derived from Freud's classical psychoanalysis and the innovations in that approach introduced by Adler, Ferenczi, Rank, and Sullivan continue to dominate most work in psychotherapy. Leaving aside semi-skilled practitioners of "wild psychoanalysis," who toss out interpretations about Oedipus and Electra complexes or infantile paranoia, the systematic application of procedures and principles derived from the classical or neo-Freudian approaches continues to be taught and employed by the leading university departments in psychology and psychiatry. Let me summarize briefly the essential ingredients of the classical psychoanalytic model. They include:

1. Free association or some form of client-generated self-expression (e.g., imagery associations);

2. A relatively neutral, empathic, and nondictatorial therapist;

3. Interpretation initially of resistances and defenses;

4. Revival with appropriate emotions of significant childhood experiences;

5. Identification and analysis of transference phenomena and exploration of dreams and fantasies;

6. Encouragement of the patient's obtaining insights about childhood fantasies or distorted perceptions of parent–child or sibling relationships;

7. Working through of recurrent defenses and maladaptive reactions;

8. Termination when the patient can identify the unique qualities of the therapist and can go on to independent self-analysis or "working-through" for the rest of his or her life.

The neo-Freudian or ego-psychology modifications of this classical approach have generally involved (a) a more direct confrontation of the patient concerning transference distortions, (b) a greater focus upon the communication process and on variations in communication between client and significant others, (c) more emphasis on current relationships as reflections of childhood distortions, and (d) a more direct use of the warmth, concern, or other personality characteristics of the therapist as part of the treatment process. This last point needs special attention. The most extensive investigation yet carried out of the psychoanalytic treatment procedure and its effectiveness has been the Menninger study. It led to the recognition that—overriding such factors as presenting symptoms, training of the therapist, and ego strength of the patient—the establishment of a good "working alliance" between patient and therapist proved to be the crucial determinant of a satisfactory outcome (Appelbaum, 1977; Horwitz, 1974).

I will deal later with some examples or issues of research evaluations of the psychodynamic orientation. As suggested above, the exigencies of the increased pressure for individualized psychotherapeutic service have led to a decline in emphasis on the classical psychoanalytic model. Except in the circles around the psychoanalytic institutes of a few major metropolitan areas, classical analysis or even the more extended personality-change approaches of the neo-Freudian analysts are yielding to combinations of the psychodynamic approach with more direct, problem-focused cognitive behavior-modification approaches. We are witnessing a shift in orientation—the model of the psychotherapist as a kind of detective searching out root causes of disturbance is being supplemented or even supplanted by the role of the therapist as an educator or perhaps a kind of skills-training coach.

## Imagery and Psychotherapy

The behavior therapies have chiefly emphasized changing the *public* personality or overt behavior patterns, while the psychodynamic orientation has perhaps overemphasized the intrapsychic or the *private* personality of wishes, fantasies, and memories. A key link between the two approaches is increasingly being forged, however, especially since both orientations are relying heavily on the imagery capacities of the individual client (Singer, 1974). The fact is that therapy generally occurs in a setting far removed from the social or physical environments in which clients ordinarily experience the difficulties and symptoms that necessitate treatment. An effective working relationship between the client and the therapist necessitates reliance on both their imagery systems: the client's for describing the situations and settings that relate to the difficulty, the therapist's for envisioning in some concrete detail the client's specific interpersonal transactions or troublesome experiences. By, in effect, training the client through imagery to practice certain types of action or to learn certain forms of self-regulation, relaxation, or thought-stopping, the therapist provides the client with a skill that may generalize beyond the immediate office to other settings (Meichenbaum, 1977; Singer & Pope, 1978). Without minimizing the advantages of in vivo practice of new behaviors, it is clear that most therapies must rely on some aspects of imagery out of practical necessity (Kazdin, 1978a).

In examining the range of treatment procedures that have emerged from the behavior therapy movement, I shall focus especially on those involving imagery, interior monologue, or role-rehearsal and simulation procedures. Operant methods, while undoubtedly effective in helping autistic, retarded, or severely handicapped clients, are less prominent in individual psychotherapy. An important feature of the imagery procedures or their variations is their relationship to the general paradigm shift in psychology from a peripheralist, drive-centered learning theory toward a centralist, cognitive or information-processing model of the organism (Singer, 1974). The further tie between imagery (as a part of the cognitive system) and the new recognition accorded a differentiated affect or emotion system (Izard, 1977; Singer, 1974; Tomkins, 1962, 1963) suggests that clinical practice need no longer be viewed as standing apart from basic psychology and the fundamental organismic systems. This trend is reflected in the emergence during the 1970s of the cognitive behavior therapy orientation. In this approach the systematic practice and rehearsal methods of the earlier behavior therapies are integrated with an emphasis on the private information-processing, imagery, and fantasy capacities of the client (Mahoney, 1974; Meichenbaum, 1977).

*Problem-Focused, Active Therapies*

Let me review briefly some of the more recent, active therapies, beginning with those more closely related to psychodynamic orientations and then moving toward the behavioral pole. As we shall see, imagery, training in self-talk and self-regulation, or related rehearsal skills run through many of these procedures. Berne's transactional analysis, for example, is extremely popular in weekend marathons. Some instances of its wide application often border on charlatanry, but it does incorporate useful elements of role playing, identification of self-defeating patterns, and rehearsal in fantasy of alternative life-styles. It assumes that everyone behaves at times as a *child,* an *adult,* or a *parent* (id, ego, superego). The problem is to ascertain when each role is appropriate and adaptive. People also crystallize their personalities around particular "games," roles that have been rewarded or that have been defensively effective in earlier times but that no longer have any payoff. These can be Alcoholic, Martyr, Schlemiel (an oafish, clumsy person), or Schlamazel (a person perennially the victim or beset by bad luck; the Schlemiel is a person likely to trip while carrying the soup, and the Schlamazel is the person on whom it is likely to be spilled.). By identifying these games, linking them to earlier experience, and encouraging patients to try new patterns, transactional therapy, in effect, meets some of the psychodynamic treatment goals. It also moves closer to behavior therapies in providing active practice for new types of movement and speech.

Gestalt therapy and the various "humanistic" approaches also involve more active methods: role playing, active interchanges between patient and therapist, trying out of expressive forms of behavior that have been avoided in the past. These methods are closer to behavior modification techniques such as "flooding," assertiveness training, or role rehearsal because they emphasize active practice with the therapist. They also rely heavily on corrective emotional experience and, to some degree, on insight, thus continuing to bear a relationship to psychodynamic theories of personality change. They involve frequent examinations of early childhood reactions' persisting into adult life. Often, through reenactment of scenes from earlier days (e.g., with the "empty chair technique," in which the client alternates between two chairs and simulates an argument between client and parent), they attempt to provide catharsis and also to identify new ways of handling comparable situations.

## European Imagery Methods

A group of psychotherapeutic procedures has evolved in Europe that attempts to treat neuroses and psychosomatic reactions and to resolve intrapsychic conflicts or modify personality traits through reliance on imagery associations. These methods can be traced to the work of Vogt and Schultz, German physicians who early in the 20th century began studying the connections between attention to bodily processes, images about the body, and specific physiological responses. Schultz developed an elaborate treatment procedure called autogenics in which the patient attempted to reduce symptoms as different as skin conditions or anxiety attacks by deep relaxation and intense imagery of scenes such as cool water running over one's arm or the heat of a fire warming one's fingertips. Schultz's methods as elaborated by Luthe and Schultz (1969) foreshadow some of the current biofeedback approaches used in the new field of behavioral medicine.

A method called the waking dream procedure in France or guided affective imagery in Germany has gradually evolved. After an appropriate diagnostic interview, a client is relaxed using a form of Jacobsen's progressive relaxation technique. Then the client is encouraged to imagine as vividly as possible being in a forest. The client must then allow a series of images to develop naturally from that scene so that, in effect, he or she engages in an imagery trip.

Each therapy session involves such an imagery trip. There is a minimum of interpretation by the therapist and no emphasis on transference. The series of imagery explorations—in a forest, along a stream, climbing a mountain, exploring a cave, looking at a family album—is viewed as providing a symbolic method for working out key conflicts. As used by the German psychiatrist Hanscarl Leuner and some of his followers, the method is rather standardized. Imagery explorations proceed through a series of basic conflict areas, each of which represents increasingly complex or potentially unconscious material. Exploring an underground cave, for example, ought to bring one into contact in imagery with some of the most primitive, id-related conflicts or difficulties.

While the mental imagery therapies seem rather exotic and almost mystical to many American mental health workers, a sizeable body of clinical literature and some fairly well-controlled studies summarized by Luthe and Schultz (1969) and by Leuner (1978) attest to the usefulness of these approaches with a variety of clinical patients. I have carried out an examination of the characteristics that these methods have in common with psychodynamic therapies (Singer, 1974, 1978). It is clear that while the imagery techniques draw on psychoanalytic notions of conflict and Jung's approach to symbolism, they also employ procedures like relaxation, positive imagery, flooding, desensitization, and symbolic modeling that are to be found in behavior modification. At the theoretical level they seem closer to the psycho-analytic or psychodynamic approach to personality change, but in practice they often resemble the systematic exercise orientation of social learning theory.

## Systematic Desensitization

This is the single most widely used method of behavior therapy. It has been widely applied to help people overcome phobias or other kinds of anxiety such as difficulties in public speaking or socializing. The method calls for the use of relaxation, or sometimes relaxation plus positive imagery, to counteract images of fearful scenes that the client produces in hierarchical sequence from least to most frightening.

## Covert Aversive Imagery

This procedure derives from techniques designed to extinguish an undesirable conditioned response—for example, heavy drinking or a sexually perverse act—by pairing it with a noxious stimulus. A drug like antabuse may be given to produce nausea in association with alcohol, or electric shock may be administered to a sexual deviant being shown pictures of fetish objects that have been arousing. Cautela and McCullough have developed the use of imagery (1978) as a substitute for shocks or chemicals. A patient with whom I worked managed to "unlearn" the most unwanted habit of being a "peeping Tom," which could have led to his arrest. With help from the therapist he practiced imagining scenes of himself contacting loathsome skin diseases in conjunction with images of himself engaging in the various steps of his voyeuristic or sexual peeping routine. Before long he had stopped having fantasies about peeking into windows, and the behavior disappeared (Singer, 1974).

## Symbolic or Vicarious Modeling

This procedure for eliminating fears or social inhibitions involves careful observation of persons one respects engaging in the behavior one would like to carry out oneself. A student frightened of actually harmless snakes may be more willing to approach or touch such a reptile if he or she sees a teacher or good friend doing so. This procedure, derived from Bandura's observational learning theory, has been extensively researched, especially in laboratory studies (Bandura, 1969). Imagining the model's actions may not be quite as powerful as direct observation, but systematic practice of such symbolic modeling has proven to be effective (Bandura, 1969; Kazdin, 1979).

## Flooding or Implosion

Flooding or implosion involves extensive and intensive practice, often in imagery, of unwanted or fearful scenes or actions. There is evidence that imagining the worst possibilities in the safety of the therapist's office reduces fear and permits the patient to engage in appropriate action. While there are some risks to this procedure (Bandura, 1969; Singer, 1974), it has been effective in some controlled research studies.

## Assertiveness Training and Vicarious Rehearsal Procedures

Behavior therapy procedures are increasingly being applied to teaching people socially effective responses. Thus the field is moving more and more toward enhancing broader personality change. A first step in assertiveness training procedures involves having people identify areas in which they believe they have suffered or lost out on opportunities because they were too inhibited to speak out or to take some clear or vigorous actions on their own behalf. Many women believe they have been raised to take a back seat to men in business situations, to underplay their intelligence, or to accept a man's decision even though they know it is wrong. Assertiveness training is widely employed with women to give them systematic practice in speaking more forcefully, making clear their needs to others, organizing and presenting their positions, and sometimes even resisting physical force. Actual rehearsals and psychodrama-like situations are employed. Sometimes rehearsal procedures may involve imagined encounters, impaired modeling, as well as role playing with the therapist or other members of an assertiveness training group (Kazdin, 1979).

## Cognitive Behavior Modification and Stress Inoculation

Increasingly, behavior therapists are recognizing that behavior change is produced not only by practicing specific responses but by shifting one's information gathering orientation or one's appraisal of situations. Meichenbaum (1977), for example, has pioneered in training individuals to cope more effectively with potential stress situations or to gain control over impulsive or rash behavior tendencies. He uses a number of methods that include training people to talk to themselves using calming phrases or language that can lead them to approach a situation more productively. Instead of at once saying, "Uh-oh, this is it again. I better scream!" the client is encouraged to try an interior monologue like "Uh-oh, this is it again. I better slow myself down and not run away. Let me take a better look around. What's really going on? Is there something here worth giving a try?" Procedures for employing distraction during pain and for using imagery to explore alternative possibilities are also included. In effect, an effort is made to provide a whole series of coping strategies that can help a person deal more effectively with specific stress situations as they arise.

It should be clear that even symptom-focused methods like systematic desensitization can lead to personality change. Kamil (1970), for example, showed that young adults who had overcome a specific anxiety also showed more signs of self-acceptance or competence as measured by a Thematic Apperception Test. Various behavior therapists have pointed to the fact that learning to overcome a fear or to change a bad habit not only helps one feel better about oneself but may also allow one to enter into new social situations that may be further rewarding and feed back greater change in self-attitudes (Bandura, 1978).

## Problem-Focused Approaches to Personality Change

Increasingly, psychotherapists are recognizing that the most generalized forms of treatment designed to deal with loose categories of personality description, such as obsessive-compulsive neurosis or hysterical personality, may not be as useful as once thought. Much of the research on the evaluation of psychotherapy supports the view that the best results are obtained when a fairly clear-cut problem has been identified and approached with reasonable specificity (Meltzoff & Kornreich, 1970).

One example of such a problem-focused orientation can be found in Novaco's (1977, 1979) analysis of anger and the consequences of its inappropriate expression or inhibition. Novaco identified specific kinds of modification procedures that would help clients not only identify where in their own daily life situations an expression of anger was useful or inappropriate but also begin to practice systematically demonstrating the emotion. A series of exercises designed to identify circumstances in which anger is useful or inappropriate is needed for particular individuals, as is specific training in expressions of anger that are effective for communicating with others but at the same time do not lead to overt aggression or violence. In this sense a problem-focused approach not only can be useful in dealing with people who are already grossly disturbed in this area but can become the basis for *preventive* treatment of relatively normal individuals who want to overcome this potential handicap in their later development or careers. Suppression of anger, even appropriate anger called for by provocation, seems to be linked to hypertension (Glass, 1977).

A similar problem-focused orientation has grown out of the research of Pilkonis and Zimbardo (1979). These investigators have been exploring the personality trait of shyness by a variety of psychological instruments and in relation to its potential hazards for the normal individual and for possible serious maladjustment. Employing psychological inventories and checking participants' responses against other questionnaires or against descriptions of actual social behavior, Pilkonis and Zimbardo have identified both a public and a private shyness. Public shyness is primarily demonstrated in group situations, in public places, or in formal settings of one kind or another. Private shyness is more characteristic of individuals in intimate, interpersonal contact and may also be evident in sexual situations. Pilkonis and Zimbardo find that these distinctions correlate with measures from Fenigstein, Scheier, and Buss's (1975) Public and Private Self-Consciousness Inventory.

Pilkonis and Zimbardo have proposed a series of recommendations for identification and treatment of problem shyness. They feel that shyness is best dealt with in a small-group setting where there may be others of both sexes with comparable difficulties. It is probably best to have cotherapists who can themselves play the part of models for various appropriate interpersonal behaviors. Pilkonis and Zimbardo also recommend occasional use of videotaped feedback so that clients can actually practice different methods of self-expression in public or more intimate situations. Clients are expected to keep records or diaries of their actual experiences and situations so that they can begin to identify typical patterns. Records become a basis for evaluating change as improvement takes place.

Specific practice is recommended for shy persons—greeting strangers, asking people for information or advice, calling up for dates, asking questions in class, and so on. Investigators have also found that many shy people have specific deficits in social skills. In effect, they have by the very nature of their shyness avoided sufficient day-to-day practice of behaviors such as smiling, nodding, taking the little digs that others offer, making various kinds of eye contact, and knowing how to begin or end conversations. Twentyman and McFall (1975) actually developed a whole series of imagery and behavioral rehearsal techniques designed to help shy young men improve their ability to ask for dates and then to behave appropriately during an actual date at college.

Pilkonis and Zimbardo (1979) conclude:

> Ideally . . . social-skills training should encourage a general "problem-solving" attitude towards feared social encounters rather than a set of highly specific skills relevant to only a single context. The technique for all difficult encounters is to decide on a "purpose" that one hopes to achieve and then to map out the steps required to reach it. . . . Different kinds of therapeutic interventions may be necessary for the publicly and privately shy. Publicly shy people, who are concerned primarily with behavioral difficulties, would presumably benefit most directly from social-skills training. Privately shy people, who focus on the quality of internal events, may require interventions aimed at changing their experience and their evaluation of their experience as well as their behavior. While they would also benefit from skills training, additional techniques seem relevant for them. For example, relaxation training might be useful for lessening both actual and imagined arousal, and cognitive behavior modification techniques might be helpful in lessening excessive self-consciousness and altering negative self-evaluations. Esteem building would concentrate on stopping negative references while increasing the frequency of self-praise. (p. 157)

The range of problems and symptoms to which problem-focused approaches have been usefully applied is quite extensive. A methodological advantage of these procedures is that their limited objectives and circumscribed techniques mean that evaluations can be carried out and effectiveness assessed more clearly.

A key feature to note, as suggested above, is that these approaches are built around a model that deals with personality characteristics as *skills* or styles rather than as traits. In effect, then, once areas of maladaptive thought patterns or social skills are identified, the therapist can form an alliance with the patient to help work out new patterns. The therapist may seem to be more active or directive but only in the limited sense of suggesting ways for the patient to practice new approaches that can then be incorporated into the patient's own cognitive and behavioral repertory. The key is *self-regulation,* not dependence on the therapist.

## Health Psychology and Behavioral Medicine

The concept of self-regulation opens the way for us to explore briefly the exciting new area now developing for the application of clinical psychology skills—the field of behavioral medicine. The recent report of the U.S. Surgeon-General's Committee on Health Promotion and Disease Prevention (1979) makes it clear that very significant progress has been made in reducing the dangers of communicable disease, once the greatest cause of illness and death. Instead, the diseases and risks to health to which Americans are now most prone are increasingly attributable to preventable situational and behavioral contingencies. Heart disease, some cancers, and related illnesses are occasioned in part by maladaptive behaviors, excessive eating or drinking, drug abuse, or smoking. A simple (but, for the United States, as yet unattained) change of daily habit in getting people to use seat belts could reduce automobile fatalities or head injuries drastically.

If we talk of behavior then we are talking of psychology! Clearly, a major burden of helping people change habits or develop attitudes and behavior styles that can prevent illness falls on clinical and social psychologists in the emerging field of health psychology. Methods for inducing patients or average citizens to develop patterns of self-care, to comply with dietary regimens, and to self-monitor maladaptive eating or drinking patterns are being extensively explored (Schwartz & Weiss, 1978).

Weiss and Shields (1980) have defined behavioral medicine as involving research into basic mechanisms through which behavior patterns play a role in epidemiology, causation, prevention, assessment, treatment, and rehabilitation from physical disorder or disease. The field as it is emerging has a healthy interdisciplinary quality, free of some of the territorial conflicts that have plagued clinical psychology in its relationship to psychiatry within the mental health domain.

Psychologists have been working on basic problems of identifying psychological characteristics of individuals predisposed to hypertension (Glass, 1977). The important discoveries during the late 1960s on the great range of possibilities for self-control of specific autonomic processes, as well as the more recent findings of self-regulation of *patterns* of autonomic processes (Schwartz, 1976), have brought mind and body together in a way hitherto only hoped for by theoreticians.

The methods generated by biofeedback research, broadened in more sophisticated ways that include training patients in relaxation techniques and in self-monitoring, particularly taking blood pressures regularly, noting their own mood changes under various behavioral contingencies, and using positive imagery to moderate stressful situations or to break the cycle of obsessional or phobic ruminations, have been employed as preventive and ameliorative approaches (Schwartz, 1980). Important research distinctions between somatic and cognitive manifestations of anxiety or between differential physiological patterns evoked by imagery-induced anger, fear, or sadness (Schwartz, Weinberger, & Singer, in press; Weinberger, Schwartz, & Davidson, 1979) are suggesting significant clinical approaches to prevention and treatment of stress syndromes and hypertension. The important work of Turk, Meichenbaum, and Genest (1981) on various techniques for dealing with pain syndromes is not only useful in ameliorating some of the distress of illness but has implications for preventing some of the secondary self-damaging psychological, behavioral, and physiological responses people show to severe pain (e.g., drug abuse or disregulatory stress reactions).

In a sense, these new developments point up many new challenges for clinical intervention. They also suggest that psychologists are going to have to start brushing up on their physiology and, indeed, learn to use physiological monitoring devices as well as psychometric ones in their assessment and treatment procedures.

# Evaluation of Psychotherapy

Many of the therapeutic approaches emphasized so far have the special advantages, on the one hand, of being closer to basic psychological research on the cognitive and affective systems and, on the other, of lending themselves to reasonable evaluation. There has been almost an explosion in the 1970s of new efforts at assessing the components of the therapeutic process, at studying outcomes, and at exploring change produced by placebos and so-called "nonspecific" factors (Kazdin, 1980). Some examples of different procedures can be cited here, but perhaps the clearest exposition of the issues and technology for studying psychotherapy has been presented in the work of Meltzoff and Kornreich (1970) and in specific chapters of Garfield and Bergin's revision of their monumental handbook (Garfield & Bergin, 1978).

## Is Psychotherapy Effective At All?

For years clinicians have been haunted by the deprecation of psychotherapy as a procedure implied in the reviews of outcome studies by Eysenck (1952, 1965). That ghost has now been laid to rest by more thoughtful and extensive reviews such as those of Meltzoff and Kornreich (1970) and Bergin and Suinn (1975).

Smith and Glass (1977) carried out a remarkable and statistically sophisticated review of the literature on the outcomes of psychotherapy. They were able to identify 375 controlled studies and classify them in terms of the differences in outcome between the intervention method (psychotherapy) or some form of behavior modification and a control condition. They were then able to calculate the extent to which psychotherapy could be shown systematically to be more effective than either some form of nontreatment or an alternative approach to ameliorating symptoms or effecting personality change.

It is apparent from Figure 1 that the average person who has been treated by psychotherapy shows a much greater likelihood of improvement than someone in a control condition. As a matter of fact, as Smith and Glass note, it is possible to argue that because the average study showed an advantage of about two-thirds of a standard deviation for treatment over control, the average client who had undergone psychotherapy was better off than 75% of those who had not obtained any help.

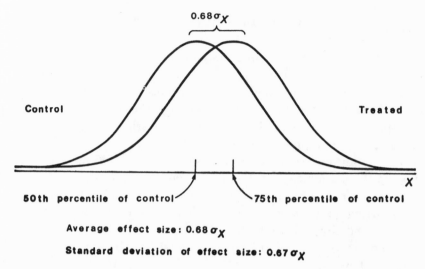

**Figure 1.** Results of a meta-analysis comparing changes in control and treated groups from 375 psychotherapy outcome studies. (From Glass and Smith, Note 1. Reprinted by permission.)

Following up on the logic of their method, Smith and Glass actually compared the size of the effects obtained in the various controlled studies across different kinds of psychotherapy. Inspection of Table 1 reveals that the strongest effects are clearly obtained from the behavior modification techniques, especially systematic desensitization. It is also clear, however, that with the exception of Gestalt therapy, most of the other treatment procedures have been yielding rather strong results and are not widely apart from each other. Although Smith and Glass are inclined to give the "Grand Prix" award to the behavior modification approaches, it might be argued that these techniques have succeeded most because they have chosen the most clearly delimited problems and have not sought somewhat broader personality change. Differences in effectiveness of types of problems or objectives of treatment are assessed in Figure 2.

Some controlled studies that have compared humanistic and behavioral approaches along with other forms of psychotherapy have been inclined to find, on the whole, relatively little advantage to the various schools, although all of the different forms of psychotherapy were more effective than no treatment at all (Luborsky, Singer, &

**Table 1**
**Grand Prix Results of Glass and Smith Meta-Analysis**

| Therapy type | Number of "effect sizes" | Average effect size ($\sigma\chi$) | Approximate standard error of the average ($\sigma\chi$) |
|---|---|---|---|
| Psychodynamic | 96 | .59 | .05 |
| Adlerian | 16 | .71 | .19 |
| Eclectic | 70 | .48 | .07 |
| Transactional analysis | 25 | .58 | .19 |
| Rational emotive | 35 | .77 | .13 |
| Gestalt | 8 | .26 | .09 |
| Client-centered | 94 | .63 | .08 |
| Systematic desensitization | 223 | .91 | .05 |
| Implosion | 45 | .64 | .09 |
| Behavior modification | 132 | .76 | .06 |

**Note.** From "Experimental Designs in Psychotherapy Research" by J. Gottman and H. J. Markman in S. L. Garfield and A. E. Bergin (Eds.), *Handbook of Psychotherapy and Behavior Change: An Empirical Analysis* (2nd ed.). New York: Wiley, 1978, p. 26. Copyright © 1978 by John Wiley & Sons, Inc. Reprinted by permission. (Data are from Glass and Smith, Note 1.)

Luborsky, 1975). Analyzing the increasing group of studies from another vantage point, Beutler (Note 2) was led to conclude that the behavior therapies are effective particularly in dealing with changing specific habit patterns, while the more cognitive-oriented therapies, which would include the psychodynamic approaches, have done at least as well with adjustment difficulties and may actually have advantages with such patients.

Goldstein and Stein (1976) also attempted a very elaborate review of studies with controls, and they looked more carefully at the specific kinds of conditions being treated. They felt the evidence was clear that techniques which focus on eliminating the motivation of an individual to maintain compulsive rituals, and which also provide rewarded opportunities for trying out other forms of behavior, have been especially effective with obsessive-compulsive individuals, a group that has on the whole been more difficult to treat.

An increasing number of very careful studies, both of dynamic psychotherapies and various behavioral or cognitive therapies, permit

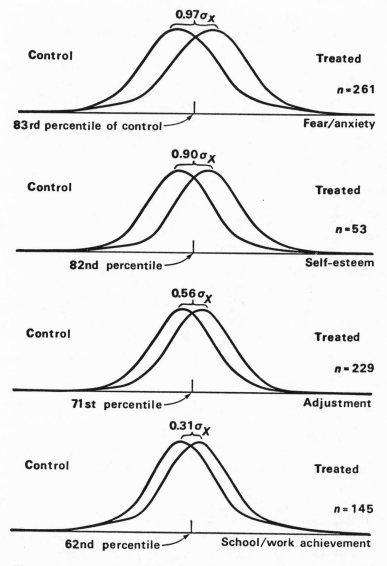

**Figure 2.** Results of a meta-analysis comparing changes in control and treated groups from 375 psychotherapy outcome studies on four types of outcome measures: fear/anxiety, self-esteem, adjustment, and school/work achievement. (From Glass and Smith, Note 1. Reprinted by permission.)

us to begin to identify the qualities of therapists and the combination of therapist and patient that might produce optimal behavioral change. For example, a well-designed study carried out at Temple University involved 90 patients who were given an extensive battery of psychological tests and assigned to two treatment groups and a control group. Six therapists, three behavioral modifiers, and three psychoanalysts treated these patients, most of whom were classified as neurotic. Detailed data were obtained from the fifth session of the treatment in order to compare the actual performance of the therapists in more detail. Follow-up studies indicated that after four months of treatment, and again a year after the initiation of therapy, both treatment groups had improved significantly more than the so-called wait-list control group. Data suggest that both dynamic and behavior modification approaches are effective, with some slight advantage for the behavior modification group. On ratings made of empathy during this study, the behavior therapists received higher scores. Incidentally, the behavior therapists offered interpretations to their patients much as the psychoanalysts did, although the content of the interpretation was different (Sloane, Staples, Cristol, Yorkston, & Whipple, 1975).

The specific advantages of a psychological intervention for modifying a severe symptom such as neurotic depression were tested in a careful study by Rush, Beck, Kovaks, and Hollon (1977). In this investigation, one group of patients received cognitive therapy designed to have them reassess the nature of their feelings of sadness and try to develop alternative ways of experiencing the daily events of their lives so that they would not necessarily lead to a downbeat reaction. In contrast, a second group received antidepression drug treatment. Care was taken to ensure that the patients were randomly assigned to the groups to avoid the possibility that patient preferences in advance might determine the outcome.

The findings of the study indicated that both drug treatment and psychotherapy ameliorated the depression to some degree. The patients' own responses to the Beck Depression Inventory and the therapist's judgment of improvement as based on various rating scales indicated that the patients in cognitive therapy improved significantly more than did the patients in drug therapy both at the end of treatment and after three-month follow-ups. A similar trend was also observed six months later. These results suggest that, despite the hopes of many medically oriented psychiatrists, there is reason to believe that effective personality change is more likely to be accomplished by a systematic and relatively focused psychological intervention.

A more active approach by therapists—more problem focused—may actually be more beneficial in producing not only symptomatic improvement but even more extensive change. For example, a study by Malan (1976a, 1976b) involved relatively brief psychoanalytically oriented psychotherapy with approximately 60 patients in a London clinic. In this case follow-ups were actually carried out more than five years after the end of treatment to find out whether changes had been enduring. It is clear from the results that the best outcome was obtained when there was an interpretive focus by the therapist on the link between transference distortions in the session and the parent/child relationships of the patient. The patient's initial motivation for changing his or her personality turned out to be a crucial consideration, as it seems to be in most forms of psychotherapy. Malan concluded that active effort by the patient for insight and what might be called a "successful dynamic interaction" yielded the best results measured over time.

## Studying the Processes of Psychotherapy

Space limitations prevent extensive exploration of the many developments in examining what happens within sessions and what technologies or combinations of patients and therapists yield the best outcomes with a particular approach. Many of these issues are extensively explored in the chapters by Gottman and Markman (1978), Luborsky and Spence (1978), and Parloff, Waskow, and Wolfe (1978), among others, in Garfield and Bergin's *Handbook of Psychotherapy and Behavior Change*. A simple example of how one can approach issues of this type with "real" clients (rather than through analogue studies) may be mentioned briefly here.

Christoph and I (Christoph & Singer, in press) sought to examine two forms of imagery that have been used as approaches to relieving phobic behavior. Clients with a range of phobias (including fears of driving, crowds, small animals, etc.) were randomly assigned to therapists who treated at least two clients each using contrasting forms of imagery: (a) an active coping scene juxtaposed with the frightening image in a desensitization hierarchy, or (b) a positive, pleasant scene (usually of a nature setting) immediately following generation of the frightening image. Mood ratings, fear ratings, and electromyographic (EMG) ratings were obtained during sessions, and scores on fear surveys and symptom inventories were obtained prior to and following treatment.

The data suggest that both types of treatment yielded significantly better reductions in phobic response than were yielded in the wait-list control group. Of special importance, however, were the indications that the positive imagery showed a more general effect, reducing reports of obsessional symptomatology more, while the coping-imagery effects were specific to the original fear. EMG results and relaxation ratings pointed to important differences within and across sessions for self-report and physiological patternings. Multiple regression analyses also suggest striking differences in the patterning of responses that predict various outcomes.

In general, we are entering a period in which careful physiological measurement, self-ratings on carefully developed scales, and other monitoring devices can be introduced into ongoing treatment procedures. These permit precise evaluation of process and outcome in individual case studies (Kazdin, 1978b) and also allow for use of large samples, various combinations of treatment approaches, or therapist–patient combinations that can then be examined using multivariate analysis methods. Generally, medical patients accept and respect the tests and measurement of physiological reactions that they must undergo in treatment. I believe patients and therapists in psychotherapy will have to get used to these approaches and will find that treatment benefits from such greater precision.

In conclusion, psychotherapy as a form of clinical intervention is alive and well. Its practice is becoming more problem focused and more susceptible to evaluation. The move toward cognitive behavior therapies has incorporated some of the important contributions derived from psychodynamic approaches to the *private* personality while applying the elements of practice, rehearsal, and skill training from earlier behavior therapies. The newer approaches to therapy, along with what we have learned about biofeedback control of bodily processes, open exciting vistas in health psychology that can be applied to prevention of disease-prone behaviors or amelioration of the consequences of established illness. Evaluation procedures include wait-list control groups who are later treated, single-case designs in which procedures can be withdrawn temporarily or alternated, studies of the processes underlying placebo or nonspecific changes, and ongoing measurement (physiological as well as psychological) incorporated into the treatment process. The use of multivariate statistical analyses increasingly permits us to look at the relative contributions to particular outcomes of client-therapist combinations, technology, and presenting complaints.

Perhaps most important of all, as I see it, is the increasing overlap between therapy practice and the basic research areas of psychology. During the 1950s and 1960s and to this day, many mental health workers were and are trained in freestanding institutes that focus exclusively on the contributions of a specific theorist. A *New Yorker* cartoon once depicted a parade down Fifth Avenue in which various groups carried banners reading, "Followers of the True Freud," "Jungians Forever," or "Gestalt Above All!" I would like to believe that the days of schismatic detachment from basic psychology are ending. Clinical practice may increasingly exemplify the best empirical research knowledge in the study of cognition, the emotions, development, personality, and social psychology.

### Reference Note

1. Glass, G. V., & Smith, M. L. *Meta-analysis of psychotherapy outcome studies.* Paper presented at the meeting of The Society for Psychotherapy Research, San Diego, California, June 1976.
2. Beutler, L. E. *Psychotherapy: What works with whom.* Unpublished manuscript, Baylor College of Medicine, Houston, Texas, 1976.

### References

Appelbaum, S. *The anatomy of change.* New York: Plenum, 1977.

Bandura, A. *Principles of behavior modification.* New York: Holt, Rinehart & Winston, 1969.

Bandura, A. The self system in reciprocal determinism. *American Psychologist,* 1978, *33,* 344–358.

Bard, M. The role of law enforcement in the helping system. *Community Mental Health Journal,* 1971, 7, 151–160.

Bergin, A. E., & Suinn, R. M. Individual psychotherapy and behavior therapy. *Annual Review of Psychology,* 1975, *26,* 509–556.

Cautela, J. R., & McCullough, L. Covert conditioning: A learning-theory perspective on imagery. In J. L. Singer & K. S. Pope (Eds.), *The power of human imagination.* New York: Plenum, 1978.

Christoph, P., & Singer, J. L. Imagery in cognitive-behavior therapy: Research and application. *Clinical Psychology Review,* in press.

Eysenck, H. J. The effects of psychotherapy: An evaluation. *Journal of Consulting Psychology*, 1952, *16*, 319–324.

Eysenck, H. J. The effects of psychotherapy. *International Journal of Psychiatry*, 1965, *1*, 97–178.

Fenigstein, A., Scheier, M. F., & Buss, A. H. Public and private self-consciousness: Assessment and theory. *Journal of Consulting and Clinical Psychology*, 1975, *43*(4), 522–527.

Garfield, S., & Bergin, A. *Handbook of psychotherapy and behavior change: An empirical analysis* (2nd ed.). New York: Wiley, 1978.

Glass, D. C. *Behavior patterns, stress and coronary disease.* Hillsdale, N.J.: Erlbaum, 1977.

Goldstein, A. *Structured learning therapy. Toward a psychotherapy for the poor.* New York: Academic Press, 1973.

Goldstein, A., & Stein, N. *Prescriptive psychotherapies.* New York: Pergamon, 1976.

Gottman, J., & Markman, H. Experimental designs in psychotherapy research. In S. Garfield and A. Bergin (Eds.), *Handbook of psychotherapy and behavior change:* An empirical analysis. (2nd ed.). New York: Wiley, 1978.

Horwitz, L. *Clinical prediction in psychotherapy.* New York: Jason Aronson, 1974.

Izard, C. *Human emotions.* New York: Plenum, 1977.

Kamil, L. J. Psychodynamic changes through systematic desensitization. *Journal of Abnormal Psychology*, 1970, *76*, 199–205.

Kazdin, A. E. The application of operant techniques in treatment, rehabilitation, and education. In S. L. Garfield and A. E. Bergin (Eds.), *Handbook of psychotherapy and behavior change: An empirical analysis* (2nd ed.). New York: Wiley, 1978. (a)

Kazdin, A. E. Methodological and interpretive problems of single case experimental designs. *Journal of Consulting and Clinical Psychology*, 1978, *46*, 629–642. (b)

Kazdin, A. E. Imagery elaboration and self-efficacy in the covert modeling treatment of unassertive behavior. *Journal of Consulting and Clinical Psychology*, 1979, *47*, 725–733.

Kazdin, A. E. *Research design in clinical psychology.* New York: Harper & Row, 1980.

Lerner, B. *Therapy in the ghetto.* Baltimore, Md.: Johns Hopkins University Press, 1972.

Leuner, H. Basic principles and therapeutic efficacy of guided affective imagery (GAI). In J. L. Singer & K. S. Pope (Eds.), *The power of human imagination.* New York: Plenum, 1978.

Luborsky, L., Singer, B., & Luborsky, L. Comparative studies of psychotherapies. Is it true "Everyone has won and all must have prizes?" *Archives of General Psychiatry*, 1975, *32*, 995–1007.

Luborsky, L., & Spence, D. P. Quantitative research on psychoanalytic therapy. In S. L. Garfield & A. E. Bergin (Eds.), *Handbook of psychotherapy and behavior change: An empirical analysis* (2nd ed.). New York: Wiley, 1978.

Luthe, W., & Schultz, J. *Autogenic methods* (Vols. 1–6). New York: Grune & Stratton, 1969.

Mahoney, M. J. *Cognition and behavior modification.* Cambridge, Mass.: Ballinger, 1974.

Malan, D. H. *The frontier of brief psychotherapy.* New York: Plenum, 1976. (a)

Malan, D. H. *Toward the validation of dynamic psychotherapy: A replication.* New York: Plenum, 1976. (b)

Meichenbaum, D. (Ed.). *Cognitive behavior modification: An integrative approach.* New York: Plenum, 1977.

Meltzoff, J., & Kornreich, M. *Research in psychotherapy.* New York: Atherton, 1970.

Moos, R. H. *Evaluating treatment environments.* New York: Wiley, 1974.

Novaco, R. W. Stress inoculation: A cognitive therapy for anger and its application to a case of depression. *Journal of Consulting and Clinical Psychology*, 1977, *45*, 600–608.

Novaco, R. W. The cognitive regulation of anger and stress. In P. Kendall & S. Hollon (Eds.), *Cognitive-behavioral interventions: Theory, research and procedures.* New York: Academic Press, 1979.

Parloff, M. B., Waskow, I. E., & Wolfe, B. E. Research on therapist variables in relation to process and outcome. In S. L. Garfield & A. E. Bergin (Eds.), *Handbook of psychotherapy and behavior change: An empirical analysis* (2nd ed.). New York: Wiley, 1978.

Pilkonis, P. A., & Zimbardo, P. G. The personal and social dynamics of shyness. In C. E. Izard (Ed.), *Emotions in personality and psychotherapy.* New York: Plenum, 1979.

Rapaport, J. *Community psychology.* New York: Holt, Rinehart & Winston, 1977.

Rush, A. J., Beck, A. T., Kovacs, M., & Hollon, S. Comparative efficacy of cognitive theory and pharmacotherapy in the treatment of depressed outpatients. *Cognitive Therapy,* 1977, *1,* 17–37.

Schwartz, G. E. Self-regulation of response patterning: Implications for psychophysiological research and therapy. *Biofeedback and Self-Regulation,* 1976, *1,* 7–30.

Schwartz, G. Behavioral medicine and systems theory. *National Forum,* 1980, *60* (Winter), 25–29.

Schwartz, G., Weinberger, D., & Singer, J. A. Cardiovascular differentiation of emotion following imagery and exercise. *Psychosomatic Medicine,* in press.

Schwartz, G. E., & Weiss, S. M. *Proceedings of Yale Conference on Behavioral Medicine* (DHEW Publication No. NIH 78-1424, 78). Washington, D.C.: U.S. Government Printing Office, 1978.

Singer, J. L. *Imagery and daydream methods in psychotherapy and behavior modification.* New York: Academic Press, 1974.

Singer, J. L. Experimental studies of daydreaming and the stream of thought. In K. S. Pope & J. L. Singer (Eds.), *The stream of consciousness.* New York: Plenum, 1978.

Singer, J. L., & Pope, K. S. (Eds.) *The power of human imagination.* New York: Plenum, 1978.

Sloane, R. B., Staples, F. R., Cristol, A. H., Yorkston, N. J., & Whipple, K. *Short-term analytically oriented psychotherapy vs. behavior therapy.* Cambridge, Mass.: Harvard University Press, 1975.

Smith, M. L., & Glass, G. A meta-analysis of psychotherapy outcome studies. *American Psychologist,* 1977, *32,* 752–760.

Tomkins, S. S. *Affect, imagery, and consciousness* (Vols. 1, 2). New York: Springer, 1962, 1963.

Turk, D. C., Meichenbaum, D. H., & Genest, M. *Pain and behavioral medicine.* New York: Guilford, 1981.

Twentyman, C. T., & McFall, R. M. Behavioral training of social skills in shy males. *Journal of Consulting and Clinical Psychology,* 1975, *43,* 384–395.

U.S. Surgeon-General's Committee on Health Promotion and Disease Prevention. *Healthy people* (USPHS Publication No. 79-55071). Washington, D.C.: Department of Health, Education, and Welfare, 1979.

Weinberger, D., Schwartz, G., & Davidson, R. The psychophysiology of low anxiety: Interactions with repressive defensiveness. *Psychophysiology,* 1977, *14,* 87.

Weinberger, D. A., Schwartz, G. E., & Davidson, J. R. Low-anxious, high-anxious, and repressive coping styles: Psychometric patterns and behavioral and physiological responses to stress. *Journal of Abnormal Psychology,* 1979, *88,* 369–380.

Weiss, S., & Shields, J. The National Institutes of Health and Behavioral Medicine. *National Forum,* 1980, *60*(1), 30–32.

WILSE B. WEBB

# THE RETURN OF CONSCIOUSNESS

Wilse B. Webb is presently a graduate research professor at the University of Florida, where he directs the Sleep Research Laboratory. After graduating from the University of Iowa in 1947 with his doctorate in experimental psychology, Webb held faculty positions at the University of Tennessee and Washington University. From 1953 to 1958 he was head of aviation psychology at the Naval School of Aviation Medicine. He left that position to become chair of the Department of Psychology at the University of Florida, a position he held until 1969. On three separate occasions he has held fellowships at Cambridge University in England.

Webb is the author or co-author of more than 200 articles in professional journals, 12 book chapters, and 5 books; most of these involve sleep research, a central focus of his for the past 20 years. Despite his heavy research commitments, he is active in a number of professional organizations including the Association for the Psychophysiological Study of Sleep, the American Psychological Association (APA), the Southeastern Psychological Association, and the Southern Society for Philosophy and Psychology. He has served as President of the latter two organizations. In addition, Webb has been President of

APA's Division on the Teaching of Psychology and has twice served terms as a member of the APA Board of Directors.

Consciousness became a topic of concern for Webb because of his continued interest in the history of psychology, and it was his sleep research that emphasized this interest. He noted, "A change in mental functioning with the onset and termination of sleep is one of the most obvious phenomena of sleep. A handy summary phrase is that there is an altered state of consciousness. While one may study a segment of a continuum (i.e., sleep) without regard to the whole continuum (i.e., consciousness), it seemed to me that some attempt to comprehend the nature of the continuum itself would be useful." In this paper, Webb weaves his interests in history, sleep, and teaching into the broad fabric of consciousness.

# THE RETURN OF CONSCIOUSNESS

I n a rapidly changing field such as psychology, age, administrative demands, or both tend to drive one's teaching into history, introductory psychology, or a microcosmic specialty: history because it tends to remain stable and recallable—one can keep up, introductory psychology because one can superficially remain at least a chapter ahead of the untutored, and the microcosmic specialty because it can be sufficiently circumscribed to maintain expertise with limited energy or time.

The G. Stanley Hall Lectures fit my aging state. Certainly age has sharpened my historical interests (I teach such a course), and my research has been intensively focused in the specialty of sleep. Furthermore, the series is about introductory psychology. And perhaps, on consciousness, I am one chapter ahead.

As we shall see, history has not been kind to the topic of consciousness. In fact, as the topic today appears in introductory courses, it is most typically a discussion not of consciousness, but of variations thereof—sleep and dreams (my microcosm) and alterations of consciousness by drugs, various meditation routes, and hypnosis. However, I hope to show that these are but signs of a quiet and certain return of consciousness as it creeps slowly back into all of psychology.

I shall begin with a brief statement about consciousness and then trace the treatment of consciousness in introductory psychology by surveying the classical texts of early psychology—prebehaviorism—roughly from the 1890s to the 1920s. Then I shall consider texts from circa 1920 through the 1950s. Roback (1964) described this latter period in his history of American psychology in a chapter titled "Psychology Out of Its Mind": "It has been observed long since that first psychology lost its soul, then lost its consciousness." I shall document the regaining of consciousness in contemporary psychology, particularly in introductory psychology texts. Finally, I will discuss sleep, dreams, drugs, hypnosis, and other altered states of consciousness and the teaching of them.

## William James and Consciousness

What is the meaning of "consciousness"? My expert on the matter is William James. And lest anyone consider this a monumental regression into the dark ages of thought, I merely ask a reading of him.

James, in the essay "La notion de conscience" in the *Archives de Psychologie* of 1905, defines consciousness as "the capacity which the parts of experience have of being reported or known." More loosely and more descriptively in his 1892 *Psychology: Briefer Course* he wrote,

> The first and foremost concrete fact which everyone will affirm —is the fact that consciousness of some sort goes on. "States of mind" succeed each other. If we could say in English "it thinks" as we say "it rains" or "it blows" we would be stating the fact most simply and with the minimum of assumptions. As we cannot, we must simply say that the thought goes on. (p. 152)

James then spelled out his famous four core characteristics of consciousness:

> 1) Every "state" tends to be a part of a personal consciousness. 2) Within each personal consciousness states are always changing. 3) Each personal consciousness is sensibly continuous. 4) It is interested in some parts of its object to exclusion of others, and welcomes or rejects—chooses from among them, in a word—all the while. (p. 152)

While these statements may be too amorphous for many or lack "operational" definitiveness, they do, I believe, well locate the ball park. I would also note that James himself described his statements as "a painter's first charcoal sketch upon his canvas in which no niceties appear." These "niceties" are later detailed in the *Briefer Course*, commented on *in extenso* in *Principles of Psychology* (James, 1890) and, in particular, probed in a major paper, "Does Consciousness Exist?" (James, 1904). (Answer: Not as a stuff but as a function.) In the end, after intensive, extensive, and often exquisite explorations, James (1890) writes:

> All people unhesitatingly believe that they feel themselves thinking [he later prefers "feeling and thought"]. I regard this belief as the most fundamental of all postulates of Psychology and shall discard all curious inquiries about its certainty as too metaphysical for the scope of this book. (p. 5)

For the moment, then, let me ask you to lay aside, with James, those lurching, lurking methodological issues of introspection, problems of reliability and elementalism, philosophical concerns about monism, dualism, interactionism, emergentism, and the soul, and philosophy of science issues of objectivity and accessibility. With me, accept the commonsensical presence of what we all know—that we think and feel and that probably others do as well.

Certainly this was the position taken in the early texts of our worthy predecessors. Not only did they accept the presence of consciousness but they considered it the primary subject matter of psychology. Following are statements from the major texts of these times.

John Dewey's *Psychology* (1886): "Psychology is the science of the reproduction of some universal content or existence. Whether of knowledge or action, in the form of individual, unsharable consciousness." (p. 6)

William James's *Psychology: Briefer Course* (1892): "Psychology [is] the description and explanation of 'consciousness' as such." (p. 1)

E. B. Titchener's *Outline of Psychology* (1897): "Everyone knows in a rough way what it is that psychology deals with. It treats of the 'mind' and 'consciousness' and the laws of the mind's consciousness." (p. 6)

J. R. Angell's *Psychology* (1904): "Mental acts or facts of consciousness constitute the field of psychology." (p. 1)

H. Carr's *Psychology* (1925): "The conscious processes constitutes the subject matter of psychology." (p. 6)

## Post-Watson Texts

While Carr had not heard the death knell of consciousness tolled, that tocsin had been clearly sounded.

J. B. Watson's *Psychology From the Standpoint of a Behaviorist* (1919): "The present volume does some violence to the traditional . . . the reader will find no discussion of consciousness and no reference to such terms as sensation, perception, attention, will, image and the like . . . I have found I can get along without them . . . I frankly don't know what they mean, nor do I believe anyone else can use them consistently." (p. viii)

The extent to which Watson and the Zeitgeist prevailed relative to consciousness—the heretofore dominant theme and concern of psychologists—is truly remarkable, and I do not think that the means or meaning of that revolution are yet known or appreciated. Consider the evidence, however. I drew from my bookcase some of the major and standard introductory texts from the 1930s through the 1950s and looked to their subject matter indexes. The results were as follows:

J. F. Dashiell's *Fundamentals of General Psychology* (1937–1949): No reference.

Boring, Langfeld, and Weld's *Foundations of Psychology* (1948): The preface contains a striking and startling statement about consciousness. "In 1948 the important thing about the organism is not that it is conscious, but that it reacts to stimulation" (p. viii). What is startling about the statement is that the senior author, E. G. Boring, had written a major book called *The Physical Dimensions of Consciousness* (Boring, 1933). He also prepared the first chapter of *Foundations of Psychology*, which contains the only reference to consciousness in the book. In that chapter, after a mention of Descartes and consciousness, Boring briefly defines consciousness as "immediate experience" and presents the petulant statement that "unconsciousness . . . has to be figured out—by yourself, your friends, your psychiatrist or someone else" (p. 7). The topic never surfaces again across the 620 pages.

N. Munn's *Psychology* (1946–1961): As he begins with a historical review, Munn cannot ignore Wundt and functionalism's concerns about consciousness, but he treats them in some five sentences. However, after noting Watson's eschewal of consciousness, it is clear where Munn stands. He describes an illustrative experiment relative to a red and green light and concludes that "the investigator of behavior is satisfied to demonstrate that an organism distinguishes between the two lights. He believes nothing is added to our scientific understanding by saying that the light produced different conscious experiences" (p. 24). Consciousness then vanished from the 797-page book.

Into the 1950s—Kimble (1956), Morgan (1956), and Krech and Crutchfield (1958) remained pristine in their indexing of consciousness. Only in Hebb do we find a slight reception, but even here there is caution.

Hebb's *Textbook of Psychology* (1958): "The word [consciousness] needs to be used with care; for many persons it means something not a part of the physical world, an attribute of an immaterial world or soul instead of a brain activity. This might be reason enough to avoid the term entirely in scientific discussion, except that [it] is needed to refer to differences between waking . . . under anesthesia, or in concussion or in deep sleep" (p. 200). Hebb then proceeds with a lucid three-page discussion of consciousness, concluding that consciousness can be considered "a complex thought process" which "determines behavior," diminishes or increases "responsiveness," and may maintain "purposive behavior" (pp. 202–204).

Surely I think that we can agree, utilizing the infallible index of "Truth, behavior," that somewhere in the 1920s and through the 1950s the introductory psychology text clearly underwent a loss of consciousness.

At this point the almost overwhelming tendency is to lapse into an analysis of the factors to which this could be attributed—the dephilosophizing of psychology, simplistic scientism, rampant behaviorism, impoverished positivism and operationalism, and so forth. But this is certainly not the time nor the place for such a self-satisfying effort.

## Contemporary Texts

Rather, let us turn again to the data base. It clearly indicates that introductory psychology may be regaining its consciousness.

Through the good services of that constant recipient of introductory texts—my department chair—I corralled a set of recent and near-recent introductory texts. They represent, if not a random or representative sample, at least an unplanned and certainly unbiased sample:

Baron, R. A., Byrne, D., & Kantowitz, B. H. *Understanding behavior* (2nd ed.). New York: Holt, Rinehart and Winston, 1980.
Coon, D. *Essentials of psychology: Exploration and application.* New York: West, 1979.
Davidoff, L. L. *Introduction to psychology* (2nd ed.). New York: McGraw-Hill, 1980.
Geiwitz, J. *Psychology: Looking at ourselves* (2nd ed.). Boston: Little, Brown, 1980.
Hassett, J. *Understanding psychology* (3rd ed.). New York: Random House, 1980.
Hilgard, E. R., Atkinson, R. C., & Atkinson, R. L. *Introduction to psychology* (6th ed.). New York: Harcourt Brace Jovanovich, 1975.
McConnell, J. V. *Understanding human behavior: An introduction to psychology* (3rd ed.). New York: Holt, Rinehart and Winston, 1980.
Schlesinger, K., & Groves, P. M. *Psychology: A dynamic science.* Dubuque, Iowa: William C. Brown, 1976.
Silverman, R. E. *Psychology* (3rd ed.). Englewood Cliffs, N.J.: Prentice-Hall, 1978.
Vernon, W. M. *Introductory psychology* (3rd ed.). Chicago: Rand McNally, 1980.

How things have changed! Table 1 presents my somewhat systematic treatment of these contemporary texts. As may be seen from Column 1, 8 of the 10 index "consciousness." In one of the two texts that did not index consciousness (Geiwitz), there are substantial sections titled "Interludes," which are devoted to the topics of sleep, drugs, and hypnosis. The other such text (Vernon) devotes 10 pages to an indexed "Altered states of consciousness." The reference in one text (Baron, Byrne, & Kantowitz) is slight and refers to Freudian "consciousness, levels of." Column 2 reveals that most texts have a chapter or a section designated by the term "consciousness" or altered states thereof. Only two do not, and again note that one (Geiwitz) contains substantial "interlude" materials. Of the remaining eight, four use the generic term "consciousness" in their heading. One (Coon) has entitled one of the seven major sections of the book "The Foundations of Human Consciousness" which includes the brain, sensation, perception, altered states (drugs and meditation), and sleep and dreaming.

**Table 1**

Consciousness and Topics in Introductory Psychology Texts

| Text | Index | Chapter or section | Topics and pages | | | |
|------|-------|-----------|-------|-------|----------|------------|
| | | | Sleep | Drugs | Hypnosis | Meditation |
| 1. Baron et al. | yes | no | 7 | 0 | 0 | 0 |
| 2. Coon | yes | yes | 13 | 11 | 6 | 2 |
| 3. Davidoff | yes | yes | 7 | 6 | 4 | 3 |
| 4. Geiwitz | no | no | 11 | 11 | 6 | 0 |
| 5. Hassett | yes | yes | 4 | 7 | 3 | 4 |
| 6. Hilgard et al. | yes | yes | 8 | 8 | 5 | 3 |
| 7. McConnell | yes | yes | 10 | 9 | 7 | 3 |
| 8. Schlesinger & Groves | yes | yes | 14 | 19 | 3 | 1 |
| 9. Silverman | yes | yes | 7 | 6 | 3 | 5 |
| 10. Vernon | no | yes | 3 | 3 | 2 | 0 |
| Median | | | 7.5 | 7.5 | 3.5 | 2.5 |

The degree and rate of change can be seen in examining the shift within one of these texts. The Hilgard, Atkinson, and Atkinson text was first published in 1953, during the period of "unconsciousness." While four pages were indexed under "consciousness," one referred to "self-consciousness" in adolescents, one referred to William James's interest in consciousness, and one defined consciousness as "self-aware-ness" and went on to say, "Psychologists are by no means unanimous as to the place of private experience (consciousness) in a science of psychology. . . . By including verbal reports . . . [they] do not exclude the study of conscious process." In the sixth edition of this text, a chapter is titled "States of Consciousness" and runs 30 pages in length.

I have noted that generally these sections emphasize "altered states" of consciousness. The remaining columns of Table 1 give a rough page count of the materials appearing in the chapters and sec-tions, or covered elsewhere in the texts. It is clear from this table that the central topics of the area are sleep and dreams (10 of 10), drugs (9 of 10), hypnosis (9 of 10), and meditation (7 of 10). I shall later give a more detailed response to these topics. Biofeedback is also included in five of the texts in association with "altered states" relative to alpha training. In the three others it is either discussed as a treatment mode or related to learning or physiology. I noted frequent references to the Sperry split-brain experiments. Although these are not generally found in the sections relating to consciousness (Coon's text is the exception), all of the texts discuss these experiments in the context of "mind" or "dual consciousness."

## The Future of Consciousness

Such an analysis indicates that "consciousness" has consciously made a remarkable comeback in introductory psychology texts. However, I believe that we are seeing the beginning of a paradigmatic revolution à la Kuhn. This infiltration of consciousness back into the introductory texts, I believe, is merely symptomatic of a widespread return to the mind and an awareness thereof throughout psychology.

Again this is neither the time nor the place for a long and learned discourse on these trends. But one cannot forebear noting recent calls for reexamining introspection (Lieberman, 1979) nor the thoughtful shifts from radical behaviorism stated by London (1972), Bandura (1974), and Lazarus (1977). A book by Pope and Singer (1978) extensively treats the stream of consciousness. More particularly, there is an impressive review by Hilgard (1980) in the *Annual Review of Psychology* titled "Consciousness in Contemporary Psychology." He points to the resurgent role of an active cognitive agent in perception, Piagetian developmental psychology, psycholinguistics, psychopharmacology, social psychology, personality, humanistic and transpersonal psychology, as well as the not yet conscious cognitive psychology. To these I would add a renewed interest in daydreams and imagery. In short, if one sniffs the wind, it is clear that the active, experiencing, knowing, conscious nature of human existence is seeping back into the behaving automaton of yore.

There are dangers here, of course. We must not be lured into stuffing humans with warm but ephemeral "ghosts in the machine." Hilgard (1980) states the matter well:

> The opening up of psychology, without sacrifice of the gains that have been made in tight theorizing and precise experimentation, is all to the good. The exploitation of the new freedom by those who have a distaste for the discipline of science will have to be guarded against, but this risk must not discourage those who have retained a curiosity about all aspects of the mind and human behavior, and at the same time are determined to retain and advance psychology's stature as a scientific enterprise. (p. 23)

What does the future hold for the teachers of introductory psychology? There seems little doubt that consciousness has a firm foothold in the introductory texts, at least via the interesting and fascinating "altered states of consciousness." There seems considerable evidence, as I view the panorama of psychological thought, that that intractable and most obvious operative force—one's awareness of oneself and one's own thoughts and states, one's consciousness—will infuse more broadly into all of the standard topics of learning, motivation, development, perception, social interactions, and personality. Future textbooks will find it increasingly difficult to "be uncertain about the place of private experience," and most will find it necessary to face up to the fact that psychology, to be satisfactory to the student, must deal not only with behavior but with experience as well.

## Teaching Consciousness Today

For the moment, at least, my starry-eyed vision of "consciousness" in introductory psychology is not extant, and I now turn to being as useful as possible to the instructors of that course. Presently, the primary dimensions of consciousness, as we have noted, center not around consciousness but around variations thereon, typically appearing as "altered states of consciousness," under which are grouped sleep and dreams, drugs, trances, and hypnosis. I must confess a lack of expertise across this scattered domain. I believe I can, not immodestly, claim expertise in the area of sleep and dreams and, through reading and research, an ancillary and competent knowledge of drugs and behavior. (After all, sleep and sleeping pills are embraced in a multibillion-dollar business.) My knowledge of trances—the various meditational types—and hypnosis exceeds only slightly that of the well-read psychologist.

### Consciousness

Before we launch into specific subareas it is meet and right that one begin from the base root of things—a personally comfortable concept of consciousness itself. Certainly I know of nothing more embarrassing as a teacher than to be bravely launched into a sea of details and find oneself without a bottom to one's boat. "Sir (or Ms.—), what do you *mean* by a "state of consciousness" (substitute at will "motive," "emotion," etc.)?

My first and foremost recommendation is to refer to the charm and wisdom of the master, William James, particularly Chapters 5 through 10 of the *Principles of Psychology* or, more briefly, Chapters 11 and 12 of the *Briefer Course*. However, for those of you who insist on modernity, we are blessed with an updating: the previously noted Hilgard (1980) chapter in the recent *Annual Review of Psychology* entitled "Consciousness in Contemporary Psychology." Oddly enough, in this review I find no definition of consciousness. Finally, if left uncertain or needing a short cut, turn to McConnell, who neatly and frankly, in two pages, asserts that consciousness is a "primitive" (elemental) given that is best defined by its characteristics and who then cites characteristics.[1]

## Sleep and Dreams

As can be seen in Table 1, all of the current texts that I reviewed have a section on sleep and dreams. These range from 3 to 14 pages (median = 7½ pages). This is a far cry from the situation in the survey that I made of books in the late 1950s. Four of those 10 texts contained no reference to sleep, and the remainder ranged from 4 paragraphs to 14. The total coverage in those 10 texts reaches the present single text median of today—7½ pages.

For background material we have gone from paucity to plethora. The number of sleep-related articles exceeds 1,500 per year. For the dedicated teacher there is an annual review published by the UCLA Brain Research Institute (*Sleep Research*) that includes an annual bibliography and meeting abstracts. The *Psychological Abstracts* indexes about 500 articles per year.

Fortunately there are several introductory-level books:

Cartwright, R. D. *Night life: Explorations in dreaming.* Englewood Cliffs, N.J.: Prentice-Hall, 1977. This book focuses on the experimental work on dreaming.

Coates, T., & Thorensen, C. *How to sleep better.* Englewood Cliffs, N.J.: Prentice-Hall, 1977. A good review of the behavioral approaches to sleep control.

[1] A more extended student-oriented "Essay on Consciousness" by the present author has been published in *Teaching of Psychology*, 1981, *8*, 15–19.

Dement, W. C. *Some must watch while some must sleep* (2nd ed.). New York: Norton, 1978. This book offers many behind-the-scenes aspects of early sleep research. The book has the further value of a marvelous set of Picasso drawings.

Webb, W. B. *Sleep: The gentle tyrant.* Englewood Cliffs, N.J.: Prentice-Hall, 1975. Broad coverage of sleep is provided in a readable fashion. The book is illustrated by Dr. Seuss.

Webb, W. B., & Cartwright, R. D. Sleep and dreams. *Annual Review of Psychology,* 1978, *29,* 223–252. A compact review of the area.

## Drugs and Behavior

Drugs are almost equal in textbook coverage to sleep (and in some books receive more coverage). Most treat marijuana, and the treatment in Davidoff and in Geiwitz is relatively extensive. In general, the treatment is "Here are the facts but they really aren't all in yet." As Geiwitz states, "It seems fair to say that marijuana is the least toxic drug ever studied. Caution is still indicated, however, as research continues. It would seem a reasonable course of action to consume in moderation, if one must consume at all" (p. 122). Alcoholism is sketchily treated and displaced out of the "drug" chapter in almost half the books. Coverage of addiction and dependence is also spotty. There is little balance relative to the therapeutic use of drugs, with tranquilizers and antidepressants being omitted (four books) or relegated to the therapy sections (five books).

There are several excellent background books in this area. My recommendations are the following ones:

Brecher, E. M. et al. *Licit and illicit drugs: The Consumers Union report on narcotics, stimulants, depressants, inhalants, hallucinogens, and marijuana.* Boston: Little, Brown, 1972.

Ray, O. *Drugs, society and human behavior.* St. Louis: Mosley, 1978. This book is particularly useful because it considers the therapeutic use of drugs.

Again, if pressed for time, I find the treatments by Geiwitz and by McConnell in the surveyed books quite comprehensive and balanced.

## Hypnosis

All except one text reviewed treats the topic of hypnosis (Baron et al.). Like drugs, this topic itself contains sufficient mystery and misconceptions that there is a reasonable tendency to play it down rather than dramatize it. Four texts give it a spare three pages or less (Hassett; Schlesinger & Groves; Silverman; Vernon). The most extensive treatments are those of McConnell and Hilgard et al. The McConnell book provides an extensive historical background and in general treats hypnosis as an unusual state of consciousness, a legitimate area of experimentation not yet fully understood. The "straightest" (most aseptic) treatment is found in the text by Hilgard, the author with the greatest expertise, and the most question-and-answer-oriented treatment is found in the text by Coon.

Three books are recommended for the subject who does not wish to rush past the topic:

Hilgard, E. *The experience of hypnosis.* New York: Harcourt Brace, 1968.
Bowers, K. S. *Hypnosis for the seriously curious.* Monterey, Calif.: Brooks-Cole, 1976.
Barber, T. X. *LSD, marijuana, yoga, and hypnosis.* Chicago: Aldine-Atherton, 1970.

## *Meditation*

This area is a child of the 1960s, forced into the psychology text by student interest and by emergent research findings. It is neatly defined in Davidoff's text as "a set of diverse exercises that aim at altering consciousness." As seen in Table 1, the topic is treated in 7 of the 10 texts reviewed. However, the most extensive treatment is only from three to four pages. Almost all of the texts focus on TM (transcendental meditation), perhaps because it appears to be the most data-oriented, but all of the texts are reserved in their treatment. Yoga is discussed in several texts in general terms. Five of the seven texts (Hassett; Hilgard et al.; McConnell; Schlesinger & Groves; Silverman) move directly into biofeedback—again emphasizing the data base.

One receives the impression that the authors sense their treatment is less than satisfying to students, and alternative readings are strongly suggested. The most frequently commended are the following:

Golsman, D. *The varieties of meditative experience.* New York: Dutton, 1977.

Naranjo, C., & Ornstein, R. *On the psychology of meditation.* New York: Viking, 1971.

Tart, C. *Altered states of consciousness* (2nd ed.). New York: Wiley, 1972.

All of the above authors are psychologists. The Tart book encompasses not only meditation but hypnosis, drugs, and dreams.

## Other Areas

The topics of sleep and dreams, drugs, hypnosis, and meditation presently constitute the bulk of the topics from which consciousness seems to be reestablishing a foothold in contemporary texts. In short, with a few exceptions, this odd group of "altered states of consciousness" constitutes a polyglot ghetto of convenience. But I am optimistic about the grand vision suggested earlier. This optimism stems from several trends I noted in my review.

First, as a trend spotter, I have noted that a topic gathering momentum is the laterality of the brain. This is typically dramatized by the split-brain findings of Sperry. The topic is presently in 8 of the 10 texts examined, and at least half treat it in a dual "mind" context. Where the "mind" is, consciousness cannot be far behind. As biofeedback becomes more of a technical treatment mode and meditation fades as a fancy, I would not be surprised to see laterality and split-brain findings become centerpieces in a discussion of consciousness.

Second, the concept of consciousness almost inevitably drifts about in discussions of motivation, personality, and Freud. If consciousness becomes consciously treated, then unconsciousness may well be coherently discussed in an appropriate context. A recent article, perhaps encouraged by the renaissance of consciousness, is bold enough to suggest that unconsciousness may well be a necessary construct for a reasonable psychology (Shevrin & Dickman, 1980). (It is interesting to note that during the period when consciousness was banished as irrelevant to behavior, unconsciousness continued as a behavior determinant in most of the texts.)

Finally, while most of the current "cognitive theories" seem to remain as unconscious as the computers on which they are modeled, at least William James and I find one aspect of consciousness so patent in its character—namely, attention—that its treatment as an aspect of consciousness seems necessary. Indeed, I suspect that the angels in heaven will sigh with relief and students nod with approval when consciousness and attention are once again discussed together.

## Demonstrations and Further Tips

Having set before you some resources, let me now turn briefly to "teaching tips" and "demonstrations" by topical areas.

*Sleep*

Sleep has three measurement dimensions: structure, patterns, and subjective aspects. Sleep structure refers to the aspects of the ongoing process of sleep and is at once the most technical. Put simply, we can effectively see 'into" sleep only by electrophysiological means—primarily the electroencephalogram. From the outside it is pretty dull.

However, the most interesting of the five stages of sleep is the so-called REM stage. REM stands for rapid eye movements, which are associated with the stage in which dreaming occurs. These eye twitches can be seen from the "outside." In adult humans they seldom occur before about 60 minutes of sleep. However, students may be advised to observe their pets or available infants, in whom these states are frequent and more apparent. In REM sleep, the subject's eyes can be seen to begin to twitch (often partially open), breathing may become irregular, and small twitching of the limbs will occur. The profoundness of the sleep can be demonstrated by lifting a limb and dropping it. In this stage there is also a profound atonia, or loss of muscle tonus.

However, I would focus on sleep *patterns*—the length and placement of sleep. These are readily accessible through sleep questionnaires or daily sleep diaries and easily permit classroom participation. The results may be used to emphasize individual differences, to rail against turning "averages" (8 hours) into norms, and to emphasize the inherent biological aspects of sleep.

My favorite demonstration relative to the subjective aspects of sleep serves also to teach a lesson about the care that is necessary in such measures. I ask the students to number places on their papers for four answers, and I then ask the following questions. Question 1: "Did you have a good night's sleep or a bad night's sleep last night?"

Question 2: "Did you have a good night's sleep, a bad night's sleep, or both a good and bad night's sleep?" Question 3: "Did you have a good night's sleep, a bad night's sleep, both, or neither?" Question 4: "Did you have a good night's sleep, a bad night's sleep, both, neither, or do you really not know?" I then have the "good/bad" answers tallied. Typically, they will have shifted from about 80% good and 20% bad on Question 1 to about 30% good and 10% bad on Question 4.

You can point out that even the remaining good/bad answers may not be homogeneous: "Good" compared to what? The previous night? The way students think other people sleep? The way they expect to sleep? And "bad" because they had difficulties getting to sleep, because they kept waking up, because it was less than they needed, or because of the way they felt when they woke up?

You can then note that a study which tried to relate, say, some personality trait like introversion to the first set of answers would likely be doomed by some 60% "false positives" and a poorly defined criterion.

I try to avoid classroom dream interpretation like the plague. I do so because I agree with Hall (1966) that a dream is like a "personal letter to oneself." More often than not a dream can only be interpreted or understood by someone who knows the dreamer intimately —the person himself or herself or a skilled practitioner. However, on occasions I would rather avoid, the meaning of a dream is painfully apparent and such public readings of private notes can be embarrassing.

I do not denigrate dreams (although I confess to having described them as the "foam on the beer of sleep"). When pressed regarding their interpretation I refer students to a bestselling book by the English psychologist and sleep researcher Ann Faraday (*Dream power*. New York: Berkley Medallion, 1973). This is a readable and useful book about understanding one's own dreams.

## Hypnosis

The first thing I would suggest is *no* demonstration of hypnosis. Early in my teaching career I made that mistake and created an epidemic of attempts (and successes) in the dormitories and fraternity and sorority houses, which ended at 2 a.m. with my coping with a hysteric. I would further note that in these modern times, the problems of informed consent and rules about human subjects are relevant to classroom demonstrations, and with hypnosis you are in a complicated thicket relative to suggestibility of subjects.

State, teach, and reiterate that hypnosis is not a parlor game but a complex research area and clinical tool. Indeed, I am loath to use the standardized suggestibility tests as a demonstration of individual differences and an established relationship with hypnosis. Too often I find this leads to questions (and self-questions) about "why" and "good or bad."

There is one "neat" demonstration. You may want to talk about "stage demonstrations" and "nonscience." A frequent "demonstration" used on the stage involves hypnotizing a subject and showing the "magic qualities" of hypnosis by having a person placed on three chairs: one under the person's head and shoulders, one under the feet and lower legs, and one under the back. When the person is asked to lift his or her body slightly while the middle chair is removed, lo and behold the person shows an amazing "hypnotic" rigidity (see Coon, 1979).

## Drugs

Again, confession time. My comments in this area are likely to be of limited use, if not counterproductive. My expertise in this area is centered on the use of drugs as sleeping pills. Here the evidence is fairly clear—in limited use they can alleviate "situational" insomnias. Carefully selected and used, drugs can ameliorate severe chronic insomnias. To date they cannot "cause" sleep or "cure" underlying sleep problems. Sleeping pills are vastly overprescribed by unwary and untrained physicians, because they offer easy "solutions" relative to sleep disorders.

This narrow base of benefits must be matched against "costs." Dollar estimates of sleeping pills average about one-half billion when over-the-counter drugs are included. But far more costly are the abuse potentials. Chronic use of most sleeping pills results in poor sleep—the cure becomes a cause of further sleep problems. Worse, most sleeping pills have been shown to have high dependency, if not addictive, characteristics as well as being lethal in high dosages. I need only point to the fact that one of the most troublesome of the "street drugs" is Quaalude, which was introduced as a sleeping pill.

As a result of this knowledge I tend to end up arm waving, sermonizing, and tearfully on my knees with pleas for mercy on our own civilized souls. And this to an audience who does not have the problem. This behavior alternates with scoldings about the nature of humankind's inhumanity to itself. Obviously, I cannot recommend this for teachers.

Furthermore, the real question in the introductory course is not sleeping pills. It is mainly "pot," with a cocked ear toward the "harder stuff" and, if you insist, alcohol. And, so far as I can make out, even if you have reservations relative to societal or personal costs, you have not got much of a chance of being heard. For those who are "into it," the personal "benefits" (including developed dependency) are unlikely to be offset by potential future personal or remote societal costs. It is somewhat like saying to a person who bought a ticket for a ski trip that it may result in a broken leg and that there are probably better ways to spend one's money. You can guess the reply: "Maybe somebody else, but not me, and if you haven't tried it, don't knock it." As for the "virginal" ones, they are already saved, and you probably have not got enough ammunition for them to shoot down anyone else.

There is one dramatic demonstration, but I cannot recommend it. You can try to give a lecture dead drunk. At the next class you can ask the students how they thought you did. Then, of course, you can lead a discussion of the diminishing effects of drugs on behavior.

## Meditation

I suspect this is a topic that will diminish in emphasis and shift in form over time. For example, while Transcendental Meditation is often mentioned in the current texts, I am reasonably sure it will wane in the new editions. However, I think that we can always count on the reemerging "promises" of the attainment of "higher levels of consciousness" and trailing promises therefrom.

You can, of course, give basic training in "meditation." The most straightforward "treatment" is that proposed by Herbert Benson, who was early associated with Keith Wallace, who became the head of the TM program. Benson concluded that the "relaxation response" represents the hard core of meditation (*The relaxation response.* New York: Avon, 1975). This exercise is comprised of four elements: quiet, a comfortable position, a passive attitude, and a "focus" such as the repetition of a word (in TM, your "mantra") usually tied in to breathing. This should be practiced for at least 20 minutes daily.

Having said that, I will now tell you what I do. But I advise *you* not to do so unless you are willing to offend some, probably a significant, part of your class and unless you have sufficient rapport with your class to survive being seen as a "scold."

I use this class period to talk about the everpresent "prey on our problems." I point to two truisms: (a) In varying degrees, we all hope that "things" (including ourselves) can be improved upon, and (b) in varying ways, "opportunities" for improvement are offered. Since needs are present and means proposed I then suggest that it may be useful to try to set up some kind of criteria to judge the probability of success in the method chosen.

Instead of using as an example the early sales of "snake oil" or "magic elixirs," I use some contemporary "behavioral program." One I have found particularly useful and pertinent for the topic of "altering consciousness" is the Transcendental Meditation program. The criteria I propose for judging the method are the following:

1. The breadth and degree of promises—the more absolute and far-ranging the promises, the lower the probability of success.

2. The universality of the population to whom offered—where there are limitations in terms of personal characteristics or resources, the lower the probability of success.

3. The training requirements of practitioners—the shorter and more specialized the program of training, the lower the probability of success.

4. The evidence of past successes—the degree to which evidence is based upon testimony or examples, in contrast to cumulative and complete data bases, the lower the probability of success.

5. The commitment required of the recipient—the shorter and more limited the commitment, the lower the probability of success.

6. The level of acceptance by the most closely associated established disciplines—while admittedly there is a conflict of interest here, the acceptance by professionals of alternative procedures must be weighed.

In short, any procedure that firmly promises successes of "helping" in a broad range of problems regardless of personal characteristics, that is offered by a narrowly trained practitioner for a limited period of time, that provides primarily testimony and examples as justification, and that is rejected by highly experienced experts in related areas should be regarded as having a dubious likelihood of success.

Since there are usually many examples around and many different prior experiences or beliefs in the class members, this approach usually evokes a lively discussion. Useful comparisons can be made to educational systems, technical programs, and psychotherapy. A major problem can occur if one veers into religion, and I must admit I duck behind a smoke screen of "personal beliefs" and "variety thereof."

## Conclusions

From an early focus on "consciousness" as the subject matter of psychology, in the early 1920s through the 1950s the topic essentially vanished. In recent texts the topic has returned. At this time it is primarily discussed under the rubric of "altered states of consciousness" and includes such subtopics as sleep and dreams, drug states, hypnosis, and meditation. This is probably just a foreshadowing of a more general return of consciousness in psychology in the future.

### References

Angell, J. R. *Psychology*. New York: Holt, 1904.
Bandura, A. Behavior theory and models of man. *American Psychologist*, 1974, *29*, 859–869.
Boring, E. G. *The physical dimensions of consciousness*. New York: Century, 1933.
Boring, E. G., Langfeld, H. S., & Weld, H. P. *Foundations of psychology*. New York: Wiley, 1948.
Carr, H. A. *Psychology: A study of mental activity*. New York: Longmans, Green, 1925.
Dashiell, J. F. *Fundamentals of general psychology*. Boston: Houghton Mifflin, 1937.
Dewey, J. *Psychology*. New York: Harper, 1886.
Hall, C. S. *The meaning of dreams* (revised ed.). New York: McGraw-Hill, 1966.
Hebb, D. O. *Textbook of psychology*. Philadelphia: W. B. Saunders, 1958.
Hilgard, E. R. Consciousness in psychology. In M. Rosenzweig & L. Porter (Eds.), *Annual review of psychology*. Palo Alto, Calif.: Annual Reviews, 1980.
James, W. *Principles of psychology* (2 vol.). New York: Holt, 1890.
James, W. *Psychology: Briefer course*. New York: Holt, 1892.
James, W. Does consciousness exist? *Journal of Philosophy*, 1904, *1*, 477–491.
James, W. La notion de conscience. *Archives de Psychologie*, 1905, *5*, 1–12.
Kimble, G. A. *Principles of general psychology* (1st ed.). New York: Ronald Press, 1956.
Krech, D., & Crutchfield, R. S. *Elements of psychology*. New York: Alfred A. Knopf, 1958.
Lazarus, A. Has behavior therapy outlived its usefulness? *American Psychologist*, 1977, *32*, 550–554.

Lieberman, D. Behaviorism and the mind: A (limited) call for a return to introspection. *American Psychologist,* 1979, *34,* 319–326.

London, P. The end of ideology in behavior modification. *American Psychologist,* 1972, *27,* 913–920.

Morgan, C. T. *Introduction to psychology.* New York: McGraw-Hill, 1956.

Munn, N. L. *Psychology.* Boston: Houghton Mifflin, 1946.

Pope, K., & Singer, J. L. (Eds.). *The stream of consciousness.* New York: Plenum, 1978.

Roback, A. A. *History of American psychology* (revised ed.). New York: Collier Books, 1964.

Shevrin, H., & Dickman, S. The psychological unconscious: A necessary assumption for all psychological theory? *American Psychologist,* 1980, *35,* 421–434.

Titchener, E. B. *Outline of psychology.* New York: Macmillan, 1897.

Watson, J. B. *Psychology from the standpoint of a behaviorist.* Philadelphia: Lippincott, 1919.